Human Resource Management in the Indian Tea Industry

Liberalization, Privatization and Globalization policy was advocated in India in 1991 under the supervision of P.V. Narasimha Rao, the then prime minister of India. As a consequence, the tea plantation industry was largely affected. It has confronted difficult competition because of the simplification of tariff barriers and the removal of the quantity restrictions on imports. The result of these on the share of export of Indian tea has declined, the price has plunged, and the profitability has reduced.

To remain competitive in the market, tea-producing companies have been forced to reduce the various costs, especially labor costs. Due to this, tea companies are not in a position to fulfil their responsibilities, such as health, safety, welfare, and good working conditions to the workers. Besides, improper recruitment of labor, lack of proper training facilities, and even irregularities in payment of wages have been increased significantly. As a result, 1.2 million workers in the tea industry, who continue to work in the industry to sustain themselves and their families, have been adversely affected. This leads to labor unrest and the industry has become vulnerable. The final impact of all these issues spreads to the quality of tea and profitability of the industry in India. This book examines the existing human resource management practices in the Indian tea industry. It adopts a simplified yet comprehensive approach to showcase workforce management in the tea industry.

This book will be of value to postgraduate students, researchers, HR professionals, and policymakers in the fields of human resource management, business history, and industrial relations.

Dr. Nirmal Chandra Roy is Assistant Professor in the Department of Business Administration (Human Resource) at the University of Burdwan, West Bengal, India.

Dr. Debasish Biswas is Assistant Professor in the Department of Business Administration at Vidyasagar University, West Bengal, India.

Routledge Focus on Business and Management

The fields of business and management have grown exponentially as areas of research and education. This growth presents challenges for readers trying to keep up with the latest important insights. *Routledge Focus on Business and Management* presents small books on big topics and how they intersect with the world of business research.

Individually, each title in the series provides coverage of a key academic topic, whilst collectively, the series forms a comprehensive collection across the business disciplines.

Innovation in Africa
Fuelling an Entrepreneurial Ecosystem for Growth and Prosperity
Deseye Umurhohwo

Consumer Behaviour and Social Network Sites
The Impact of Negative Word of Mouth
Sarah Zaraket

Artificial Intelligence in Accounting
Practical Applications
Cory Ng and John Alarcon

Digitalised Talent Management
Navigating the Human-Technology Interface
Edited by Sharna Wiblen

Human Resource Management in the Indian Tea Industry
Nirmal Chandra Roy and Debasish Biswas

For more information about this series, please visit: www.routledge.com/ Routledge-Focus-on-Business-and-Management/book-series/FBM

Human Resource Management in the Indian Tea Industry

**Dr. Nirmal Chandra Roy and
Dr. Debasish Biswas**

Routledge
Taylor & Francis Group

NEW YORK AND LONDON

First published 2021
by Routledge
52 Vanderbilt Avenue, New York, NY 10017

and by Routledge
2 Park Square, Milton Park, Abingdon, Oxon, OX14 4RN

Routledge is an imprint of the Taylor & Francis Group, an informa business

Library of Congress Cataloging-in-Publication Data
A catalog record for this book has been requested

ISBN: 978-0-367-67907-1 (hbk)
ISBN: 978-1-003-13333-9 (ebk)

Typeset in Times New Roman
by Apex CoVantage, LLC

This book is dedicated to the readers

Contents

Figures and Tables

Figures

Tables

Acknowledgments

First of all, we are grateful to all the managers, assistant managers, trade union leaders, labor welfare officers, staff members, and workers of different tea estates of the North Bengal region.

We offer our sincere thanks to the officials of the Tea Board of India's regional office of Jalpaiguri and the librarian of the University of North Bengal for their wholehearted cooperation for this study.

We also thank Mr. Chandan Dasgupta (joint labor commissioner, North Bengal Zone, Government of West Bengal) and Mr. Kollol Duta (deputy labor commissioner, Regional Labour Office, Alipurduar, Government of West Bengal), for extending their helping hands in conducting this empirical study.

We thank all the research scholars and teachers of the Department of Business Administration of Vidyasagar University for their advice and suggestions in this work.

We owe a lot to the authorities of the Vidyasagar University and the University of Burdwan of different librarians and all those who inspired and helped us in this work.

Last but not the least, we must acknowledge our deep gratitude to our parents and other family members for their continuous support and encouragement to complete this study.

The responsibility for errors is remained us alone.

Dr. Nirmal Chandra Roy
Dr. Debasish Biswas

Foreword

Drinking tea is said to be more than 4,000 years old and the credit for introducing it as a beverage goes to China. This crop is now grown in more than 50 countries throughout the world from Georgia 43°N latitude to Nelson (South Island) in New Zealand 42°S latitude and from sea level to 2300 meters above mean sea level (MSL).

In some major tea-producing countries like Sri Lanka and Kenya, tea industry is central to the national economy. In India too, tea industry has a significant place. The possibility for growing tea in India was discovered in 1824, when the Indian variety of the tea plant *Camellia* species was found growing in Assam. Inspired by its success, Dr. Campbell, the first collector of Darjeeling, attempted to grow tea in the Darjeeling hills in 1845. After Darjeeling, the Terai area in the foothills became the natural choice, and the first tea garden in the Terai was set up in 1862. But to meet the fast-growing demand for tea, more land was needed and the plains of the Dooars in Jalpaiguri seemed to be suitable for it. In 1874, Richard Houghton set up the first tea garden of the Dooars at Gajaldubi. By 1877, lease was granted to 22 gardens and more gardens were set up in the next few years.

The tea industry is one of the oldest of the organized manufacturing sectors in India and, because it is labor-intensive, it is the single largest employer within this sector. India is also the largest producer and consumer of tea in the world. However, exports of Indian tea are the lowest among the other major tea-producing countries, like Kenya, Sri Lanka, and China.

After globalization, Indian tea is facing challenge in terms of both cost and quality of the product. Challenges before this industry are really serious, and the responsibility to confront the challenges and convert them into opportunities lies with the management of the industry. Unlike modern industry, workers in the tea industry are traditional in attitude, with low levels of modernity, education, and training.

It is well recognized that progressive HRM practices can have lasting impact on the performance of any industry. Many studies have documented the relationship between specific HR practices and critical outcome measures such as productivity, product and service quality, and cost control. Effective training and development policies improve the performance of employees. Appropriate incentive and compensation systems result into higher productivity and performance. The fair treatment of employees produces greater loyalty, higher performance, and reduced costs.

Against this backdrop, Dr. Debasish Biswas and Dr. Nirmal Chandra Roy have written this book, which gives comprehensive coverage of the entire tea industry in India. In the first chapter they give a bird's eye view of the Indian tea industry and its various components with special reference to the tea estates in North Bengal. In the second chapter they trace the history of tea industry in India, again with special emphasis on North Bengal. The growth and development of tea industry in India as well as in North Bengal is described in the third chapter of the book. Against this general backdrop of the tea industry, the fourth chapter deals with the HRM practices prevailing in this industry. The fifth chapter focuses on the training and compensation practices of the tea estates in North Bengal. The final chapter highlights the integration and maintenance functions, which includes industrial relations and labor welfare.

This is a comprehensive work on the tea industry in India with special reference to the tea estates in North Bengal. It will be of immense help not only to the researchers, scholars, and academicians but also to other stakeholders of tea industry, like the employers, trade union leaders, social activists, policymakers, and labor administrators. The authors must be thanked for their hard work in making this publication, which surely will become a collector's item for anybody who is interested in the tea industry.

Kallol Dutt
Joint Labour Commissioner Government of
West Bengal North Bengal Zone

Preface

Management of human resources is one of the most important aspects and has become a deep concern for the management of an organization. The human resource of an organization comprises the entire labor force. The winning of an organization largely depends upon human resources. Human resources are the most important assets of an organization. Unlike many other resources, such as materials, technology, etc., that can be purchased and sold easily, human resource is a ticklish and sensorial element that needs to be handled with care. Even in this robotic, automation, and internet era, human resource is always a precious and unique resource. It is the people who can get other resources moving. Among all the resources of a typical organization, the major six resources are man, money, material, machine, method, and market (6 M's). If you have five all major resources except man, it's a big question that 'who will manage all these?' No organization can produce outputs and render services without proper utilization of human resources.

In India, the tea plantation industry was materially initiated and shaped by European entrepreneurs. In 1823, Robert Bruce discovered the indigenous tea plants in Sibsagar of Assam. Shortly after, tea cultivation was introduced in full swing in Assam and in the northern part of Bengal. A total of 276 organized tea estates of North Bengal play a monumental role in the economy of this region. The industry provides 2,62,426 employments directly and several million indirectly. There are 7 employers' associations and 22 trade unions registered under the banners of different political parties.

However, in recent years the overall scenario of the tea industry is not satisfactory. Several tea gardens have been closed, whereas several others have been locked out. As a consequence, hundreds of people have died due to starvation and malnutrition. These have been studied as the ill effect of the LPG (liberalization, privatization, and globalization) policy, which was advocated in India in 1991. The Indian tea industry has confronted stiff competition in the global market due to the lessening of import tariff barrier and withdrawal of the quantity ceiling on import. Thus, to remain competitive in the economy, tea-producing companies of the North Bengal have been forced to sink the various costs, especially the labor cost. Due to the cost diminution policy, tea-producing companies in this province are not in a position to execute their responsibilities, viz. health, welfare, safety, working conditions, etc., to the workers in conformity with the Plantation Labour Act (PLA), 1951. Besides these, inappropriate staffing, passive attitudes of planters on providing proper training, abnormality in payment of wages, bonus, gratuity, provident fund, etc., have increased significantly. Further, other non-statutory benefits for workers like fuels, umbrella, slippers, tarpaulin, etc., have been fully eroded.

Thus, the study concludes that the labor forces, i.e., human resources, are not properly managed in the tea plantation industry of Bengal. As a result, workers who are engaged with the tea industry for the survival of themselves and their families have been unfavorably affected. As a consequence, workers backed by the trade union call a strike and create stress on the management to execute their demands. Hence, labor conflict has become a usual phenomenon in this region. Finally, all these issues lead to labor turbulence in the forms of strikes, gheraos, etc., and thus the industry has become vulnerable.

1   Tea Industry in India

Introduction

The word 'Tea' originated from the Chinese ideograph pronounced as 'tay'. Later in the 18th century in English, the present pronunciation was converted (Mitra, 2012). According to legend, the Queen of Beverage (tea) was discovered first in China by the fabled Chinese monarch cum herbalist Sheh Nung, in 2737 BC (Mitra, 2010). The tea industry of India may be traced back to 1823, when the homespun tea plant was discovered in Assam by Robert Bush, a Scottish adventurer (Banerjee and Banerjee, 2009).

In India, the tea plantation industry was materially initiated and shaped by the European entrepreneurs (Sarkar, 2008). Essentially, the requirement of seed capital to establish the tea industry in India was injected by the UK. Thus, the industry was dominated in terms of management and ownership by the colonials. However, World War II brought about significant changes in the industry in the area of management and ownership patterns. The war incited the Indian entrepreneurs to start new ventures. During the war, Indian entrepreneurs produced a large variety of goods that were required for the war efforts. The encouraged Indian entrepreneurs then entered into venturing in tea. There was another factor behind it. During the war, a large number of workers and staff members were shifted from the tea industry for the construction of bridges, airfields, roads, and also for assisting the armed forces. Thus, the industry faced a shortage of workers and staff to produce tea. All these factors made a big challenge for foreign companies to maintain their business. During this point of time, some foreign tea companies changed their ownership into Indian companies.

As per investment is concerned, the plantation sector offers more employment in India. The tea industry has given direct employment to 12,57,610 workers (Tea Digest, 2004) and several millions of people in an indirect way. One of the unique characteristics of the tea industry is that it employs more women workers. In India, tea is grown in 5,79,353 hectares areas which are around 16 percent of the total tea cultivation area in the world.

The tea industry occupies a predominant position in the Indian economy. Tea is the most common and the cheapest beverage in India.

According to the recent report published by the Tea Board of India (TBI) in 2017, India occupies the second position in the world in terms of tea production, which is just after China. India produced around 23 percent and China produced 43 percent of the global production of tea in 2016 (Shown in Figure 1.1). India also occupies the fourth position as an exporter of tea and exported 12.19 percent of total tea export in the world market in 2016 (Shown in Figure 1.2). It is important to record that around 80 percent of tea produced in India is consumed within the country. Out of the entire tea production in India, the North Indian tea industry produced 1008.56 million kilograms, whereas the production of

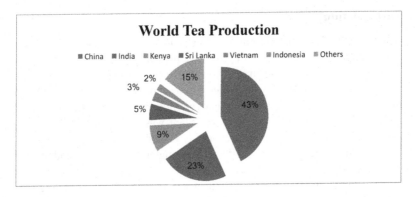

Figure 1.1 World Tea Production Share During 2016

Source: Combination of various statistics Tea Board of India (2017).

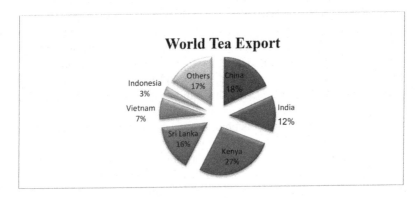

Figure 1.2 World Tea Export Share During 2016

Source: Combination of various statistics of Tea Board of India (2017).

Table 1.1 Production of Tea and Area Under Tea Cultivation in India

Tea-Producing State	Area (in hectare)	Production (in million kg)
Assam	3,22,214	652.95
West Bengal	1,15,095	329.70
Others	22,304	25.91
NORTH INDIA	4,59,613	1008.56
Tamil Nadu	80,462	161.49
Kerala	37,137	56.63
Karnataka	2,141	6.46
SOUTH INDIA	1,19,740	224.58
ALL INDIA	5,79,353	1233.14

Source: Combination of various statistics of Tea Board of India (2017)

North Bengal, which comprises Terai, Dooars, and Darjeeling regions, were 329.70 million kilograms in 2016.

However, in India, 97.36 percent tea is being produced by the four major tea-producing states, viz. Assam (52.95 percent), West Bengal (26.73 percent), Kerala (4.59 percent), and Tamil Nadu (13.09 percent). The other tea-growing states' contribution is little (2.62 percent). These states are Arunachal Pradesh, Bihar, Himachal Pradesh, Manipur, Mizoram, Nagaland, Sikkim, Tripura, and Uttrakhand. North Indian tea industry's contribution is 82 percent, whereas the contribution of the South Indian tea industry is 18 percent during the year 2016 (Shown in Table 1.1). In India, as per the geographical location, the tea industry has been divided into two regions: the tea industry of Northern India and the tea industry of Southern India. The northern parts of Bengal and Assam are the major tea-producing areas of the North Indian tea industry. Dooars, Terai, Darjeeling, Cachar, Darrang, Dibrugarh, Sibsagar, etc., are the prime producing regions of tea in North India.

In the financial year 2015–16, India produced the highest tea production in its history which is 1,233 million kilograms and exported around 232 million kilograms which valued at Rs. 4,493 crores. This record quantity of export was observed after 35 years. Earlier, in 1980–81, India exported 231.7 million kilograms of tea.

Contribution of Small Tea Growers (STGs)

The tea industry in India is composed of big or organized and small tea growers. Small tea growers (STGs) are unorganized. The Tea Board of India (TBI) defines STGs as that which has an area of tea plantation within

Table 1.2 Comparative Scenario of Small Tea Growers and Big Gardens in India

Parameters	Small Growers (within 10.12 ha.)	Big Gardens (>10.12 ha.)	Total
No. of gardens	1,80,448	1,472	1,81,920
Area under tea (ha.)	1,64,306	4,15,047	5,79,353
Production (M.kg)	584	701	1,285
Percent share in total area	28	72	100
Percent share in production	45	55	100

Source: Combination of Data from Tea Board of India and Krishi Jagran.

10.12 hectares or 25 acres of such plantation land. On the other hand, the West Bengal Land Reform Department considers small tea growers as, those having plantations within 9.79 hectares or 24.20 acres of tea culti-vated land.

The tea sector of India is going to occupy by the unorganized small cultivators. As of now, the small tea grower section contributes about 45 percent of the total tea production in India (Shown in Table 1.2). It is expected that shortly, the small tea sector's share will be more in the Indian tea industry. In Tamil Nadu, the share of small tea growers has been observed as the highest (53 percent), followed by West Bengal (40 percent) and Assam (27.6 percent). The small tea growers in India are socially and economically vulnerable as they are marginal farmers from the socially backward community. In some parts of Northern India, they do not possess the rights on land in which they are cultivating. In India, the number of small tea growers is around 3,00,000 (Chakroborty, 2018). On average, small tea growers possess tea cultivation land of two acres or less. The most common feature of these small tea growers is that they do not have any manufacturing unit of their own.

Development of Tea Industry After Independence in India

The effects of manifold policies and legislations of the government passed since independence in India on the tea industry have been summarized as follows:

Structural development of the Indian tea industry in terms of management and ownership pattern took place when the Act related to issue capital and control was implemented in 1947. As per this Act, all joint-stock companies are required to take permission for issuing of bonus on all kinds of securities and issues of capital. In this situation, many foreign companies transferred their ownership to the Indian company.

The Foreign Exchange Regulation Act, 1947, and Export-Import Control Act, 1947, also brought changes and structural development in the Indian tea industry. As per these Acts, restrictions were made on foreign exchange as well as commodity import. Thus, some of the foreign tea companies faced great difficulties to maintain and expand their business. Finally, they sold their tea estates to Indian nationals.

The minimum Wage Act, 1948, and Factories Act, 1948, also had various impacts upon the tea companies in many ways. The provisions of the Minimum Wage Act reveal that wage for the workers is to be notified and fixed by the appropriate government from time to time. On the other hand, the Factories Act mentions in its various provisions that the working hours and other statutory provisions on health, welfare, and safety might be reasonable. However, the foreign companies feared that implementation of the Act will lead to lower profitability. Thus, many foreign tea companies converted into an Indian company.

The enactment of the Plantation Labour Act, 1951, was one of the remarkable issues on the structural development of the Indian tea industry. The Act made it compulsory that in case of a tea plantation with more than 25 acres of land and employing 30 people or more, the authority must arrange suitable drinking water, latrines, and urinals, hospitals and dispensary, housing, recreational facilities, educational facilities for the child worker, etc. The foreign tea companies were largely affected by this Act, and they realized that their company might not be able to earn the profit. Therefore, they also changed ownership and management.

Thus, the Indian tea industry developed in the form of ownership patterns and management. The developed structure of ownership patterns of the Indian tea industry emerged as private limited, public limited, proprietary concerns, and partnership firms.

The Tea Board of India

The Tea Board of India (TBI) was set up on 1 April, 1954. It was constituted under section 4 of the Tea Act in 1953 under the control of the Ministry of Commerce and Industry, Government of India. TBI was established to promote, process, trade as well as export Indian tea. This is the apex body which was given the responsibility to look after the entire interest of the tea industry. TBI consists of 30 members and a chairman, appointed by the government. The head office of TBI is located at Kolkata. It has 16 regional offices (Siliguri, Kurseong, Jalpaiguri, Agartala, Tezpur, Jorhat, Palampur, Cochin, Coonoor, Silchar, Mumbai, Chennai, New Delhi, Guwahati, Dibrugarh, and Kottayam) across India and three offices abroad (Dubai, London, and Moscow). TBI performs a wide array of functions. The functions are summarized below:

  i. Rendering technical and financial assistance to the tea cultivators;
 ii. Marketing and export promotion of tea;
iii. Research and development initiatives for enhancement of production and quality of tea;
 iv. Providing monetary assistance to the workers and their family members through welfare schemes;
  v. Encouraging the small tea growers through financial and technical assistance;
 vi. Managing well the statistical data and publishing them from time to time;
vii. Promotion for potential tea market, promotion of different tea brand, and quality improvement of tea;
viii. Organizing the sellers and buyers meets, promoting the cooperative efforts, organizing campaign for promotion, and promoting Indian tea in the foreign market;
 ix. Providing licenses for export, shipment, and warehousing.

South Indian Tea Industry

The credit goes to Dr. Christie for initiating the cultivation of tea on an experimental basis at Nilgiri in 1832. Initially, tea plants were distributed to the various parts of the Nilgiri Hills for trial purposes. Cultivation of tea was taken up from the year 1853 onward in the remote hill areas of Kerala and Tamil Nadu. Further, in Karnataka, tea cultivation was also taken up in small capacity. Later in 1893, it was shaped into an industry. In 1894, the United Planters Association of South India (UPASI) was established. It was only the prime representative organization of the southern part of the Indian tea industry. The central objectives of this organization were to bring unity among the managers and owners of tea estates, and to haggle with trade unions and governments. However, the South Indian tea industry contributes about 19.57 percent to the entire tea production in India (Show in Table 1.3).

The main tea-growing regions of South India are Tamil Nadu, Karnataka, and Kerala. In Tamil Nadu, tea is grown mainly in Valparai, which is in the Coimbatore district. There are some other districts in the state where tea is grown in small capacity: Tirunelveli, Madurai, and Kanyakumari. Idukki, Kollam, and Wynaad are the key tea-producing regions in Kerala. In Karnataka, tea is cultivated in little areas; these areas are Hassam, Chickmagalur, and Coorg districts (Shown in Table 1.4). However, the

Table 1.3 Position of South Indian Tea Industry in the Indian Tea Industry

Basis	South India	India	Percent share in Indian tea industry
Production (Million kg.)	241.36	1,233.14	19.57
Area (Hectare)	1,19,740	5,79,353	20.66
Average Auction Price	85.64	142.91	—

Source: Combination data of Tea Board of India (2017).

Table 1.4 Tea-Growing Areas in South India

SL. No.	Tea-Growing Areas	SL. No.	Tea-Growing Areas
1	Wayanad (Kerala)	7	High Wavys (Madurai District, Tamil Nadu)
2	The Nilgiris (Tamil Nadu)	8	Trivandrum (Kerala)
3	The Anamallais (Coimbatore District, Tamil Nadu)	9	Singampatty (Tirunelveli, Tamil Nadu)
4	Nelliampathy (Palghat, Kerala)	10	Coorg (Karnataka)
5	High Range (Iddukki District, Kerala)	11	Hassan (Karnataka)
6	Vandiperiyar and Peermade (Iddukki District, Kerala)	12	Chikmagalur (Karnataka)

Source: Authors Created.

entire tea-producing regions of South India are divided into two geographical regions:

i.   The Blue Mountain: This particular area is popularly known as Nilgiri. The area has an average of 2,000 meters elevations and is located in South Tamil Nadu, and
ii. The Western Ghats of Kerala.

North Indian Tea Industry

The British naturalist Sir Joseph Bank was the first person who suggested the feasibility of tea cultivation in Assam, India, in 1778 (Karmakar and Banerjee, 2005). In 1819, David Scott, the then Governor-General of Assam, initiated to cultivate tea in Assam but no avail was recorded. In 1823, Robert Bruce discovered the indigenous tea plants in Sibsagar of Assam. Shortly after, tea cultivation was introduced in full swing in Assam and the Northern part of our country. The North Indian tea industry comprises Assam, West Bengal, Arunachal Pradesh, Bihar, Himachal Pradesh, Manipur, Mizoram,

Nagaland, Sikkim, Tripura, and Uttrakhand. The contributions of Assam and West Bengal are the primes of the North Indian tea industry; these two tea-growing states contribute around 80 percent of the total tea production in India. The remaining tea-growing states contribute a little, only about 2 percent to India's total tea production. A brief description of the major tea-producing regions of the North Indian tea industry is presented in the following sections.

Assam

In the Indian tea industry, Assam plays a significant role as a tea producer. The Tea Industry of Assam is the highest producer of tea in India. Half of the country's tea production comes from Assam. During the financial year 2015–16, the total tea production of Assam was 652.95 million kilograms, which were 52.95 percent of the total tea production in India. Both on production and the area of production, Assam occupies the topmost position in India. Including small and big producers, tea is cultivated in 3,22,214 hectares land in Assam, which is 55.61 percent of the total tea cultivation land in India. The main tea-producing regions in Assam are broadly divided into two distinct areas. These are:

i. **The Brahmaputra Valley:** The rich alluvium land of Brahmaputra River valley diffused from Goalpara to Sadiya is the prime tea-producing province in Assam and India. The valley contributes around 45 percent of total tea production in India, and the valley occupies around 40 percent tea cultivation area of the country. In this valley, a total of 676 organized tea estates are there in the districts of Lakhimpur, Dibrugarh, Darrang, Sibsagar, Nagaon, Kamrup, and Goalpara.

ii. **Surma Valley:** It is the second most important tea-growing area in Assam. The valley lies in the Cachar district in Assam. About 5 to 6 percent of the total tea production in India originates from here. The valley also holds around 10 percent of tea cultivation land in India. Tea gardens in this valley are scattered across small mounds, which are called *teelas* or *bheels*. The valley has perfectly drained along the river Surma and also its tributaries. The average rainfall of this valley is 300–400 centimeters and the rainfall happens throughout the year.

West Bengal

West Bengal occupies the greatest position in the tea map of India. The contribution of West Bengal to the Indian tea industry in terms of production is 26.73 percent. During 2015–16, West Bengal produced 329.70 million kilograms of tea from 1,15,095 hectares of tea cultivation land.

Brief Profile of Tea Industry of North Bengal

The tea industry of North Bengal lies under the Himalayan foothills and covering the districts of Alipurduar, Jalpaiguri, Darjeeling, North Dinajpur, and few parts of Coochbehar in West Bengal. Technically, the entire tea-producing areas in Bengal have been divided into three regions viz. Terai, Dooars, and Darjeeling hills. Terai covers the area of the Siliguri sub-division of Darjeeling district and a few parts of Uttar Dinajpur district. Darjeeling hills cover Kurseong, Kalimpong (now it is an independent district), and Darjeeling Sadar of the Darjeeling district. Dooars widely covers Jalpaiguri, Alipurduar, and a little part of Coochbehar district. Dooars is the biggest tea-producing area in Bengal and even in North India.

A total of 276 organized tea estates of North Bengal play a monumental role in the economy of this region. The industry provides 2,62,426 direct employments Government of West Bengal (2013) and several million indirect employments. There are 7 registered employers' associations and 22 registered trade unions under the banners of different political parties. A brief description of tea-growing regions of North Bengal is presented as follows:

i. **Darjeeling Hills:** Darjeeling is well known all over the world for its most exquisite aromatic tea. The annual average rainfall of around 300 centimeters, moderate temperature, and fertile soils provide special flavor to the tea. Although yields per hectare are quite low in Darjeeling, which is generally below 15 quintals/hectare, the total number of tea estates in the Darjeeling Hills is 81. Out of the 81 tea estates, Darjeeling sub-division has 46 tea estates, Kurseong sub-division has 29 tea estates, and Kalimpong sub-division has 6 tea estates.

ii. **Dooars:** The Himalayan foothills covered the districts of Jalpaiguri, and the newborn district of Alipurduar in the northern part of Bengal is popularly known as Dooars. Dooars has no political identity but geographical existence only. The name Dooars is derived from the word 'doors'—i.e., 'doors to Bhutan' (Saha and Ghosh, 2013). Dooars is the entrance to Bhutan and Northeast India. In the west, it stretches from the river Teesta. In the east, it stretches from the river Sankosh. It is situated over an area of around 130 kilometers by 50 kilometers. Dooars is bounded by two international borders: Bangladesh towards the South and Bhutan in the northwestern side. It is also bounded by one national border: Assam. Dooars has 150 tea estates.

iii. **Terai:** The 'Terai' (moist land) of Bengal has an area of boggy grass-
      land, savannahs, and forest at the foot of the Darjeeling Himalaya lying
      up to 38 kilometers southward the plain. The eastern part stretches up
      to the bank of the Teesta. Terai has 45 tea estates.

Number of Tea Estates in North Bengal Region

The number of tea estates of the tea industry in the North Bengal region is
spread over in Alipurduar, Darjeeling, Jalpaiguri, and Kalimpong districts.
There is only one set of tea estates in the district of Cooch Behar. However,
tea-producing areas of North Bengal are divided into three regions (Darjeeling hills, Terai, and Dooars). These tea estates have been presented on the
basis of sub-division in Table 1.5:

Table 1.5 Tea Estates in North Bengal

Tea-Producing Areas in North Bengal	Sub-divisions	Tea Estates	Total
Darjeeling Hills	Darjeeling	46	**81**
	Kurseong	29	
	Kalimpong	06	
Terai	Siliguri	45	**45**
Dooars	Jalpaiguri	33	**150**
	Malbazar	56	
	Alipurduar	61	
Total			**267**

Source: Combination data of Labour Department (Government of West Bengal), 2013.

Categories of Tea Estates

There are mainly three types of tea estates in the North Bengal region of the
Indian tea industry. These are as follows:

  i. Organic tea estates: 50 tea estates produce organic tea.
 ii. Inorganic tea estates: 210 tea estates produce inorganic tea.
iii. Both, organic and inorganic, tea estates: 13 such tea estates produce
      both organic as well as inorganic tea.

Table 1.6 Types of Tea Produced in North Bengal

Sl. No.	Type of Tea	Number of Tea estates in Darjeeling Hills	Number of Tea estates in Dooars and Terai	Total Tea Estates
1	CTC	01	161	162
2	Green	00	10	10
3	Orthodox	60	00	60
4	CTC + Green	01	21	22
5	Green + Orthodox tea	18	00	18
6	CTC + Green + Orthodox	00	01	01
Total		80	193	273*

Source: Combination data of Labour Department, Government of West Bengal (2013).

*Due to the suspension of work in three tea estates, survey was not conducted, and the actual number of tea estates is 276.

Types of Tea

Tea estates of the North Bengal region produce mainly three types of tea: curl, tear, and curl (CTC), orthodox, and green. In Table 1.6, a summary of various types of tea produced by tea estates has been presented.

References

Banerjee, G., and Banerjee, S. (2009). *Tea industry in transition.* New Delhi, India: Abhijeet Publication, p. 25.

Chakroborty, B. G. (2018). Khudra cha chaser abong cha silpar bhobiswat. *Krishi Jagaran (Bengali Version)*, 3(2), pp. 23–26.

Government of West Bengal. (2013). *Synopsis on survey of tea gardens.* Kolkata, India: State Labour Institute, WB, pp. 5, 13, 17.

Mitra, D. (2010). *Globalization and industrial relations in tea plantations.* New Delhi, India: Abhijeet Publication, p. 13.

Mitra, S. (2012). *Globalization: Its impact on industrial relations in tea plantation of Terai and Dooars region of West Bengal* (Unpublished master's thesis). University of North Bengal, Darjeeling, India, p. 1.

NABARD (2005). *The tea industry in India: A survey* (Occasional paper—39). Mumbai, India: Karmakar, K. G., & Banerjee, G. D., p. 1.

Saha, S. P., and Ghosh, A. G. (2013). *The development of tea industry in the district of Jalpaiguri, 1869–1968.* Siliguri, India: NL Publishers, p. 9.

Sarkar, K. (2008). Globalization, restructuring and labour flexibility in tea plantations in West Bengal. *The Indian Journal of Labour Economics*, 51(4), p. 643.

Tea Board of India. (2004). *Tea digest.* Retrieved from: http://www.teaboard.gov.in/TEABOARDPAGE/MjE5Mg==

Tea Board of India. (2017). *World production.* Retrieved from: http://www.teaboard.gov.in/pdf/Global_tea_statistics_pdf4619.pdf

2 History of Tea Industry in India

Particularly North Bengal Region

Origin of Tea

The history of tea is encompassed by the fuzzy legends and fabled tales of the fanciful Chinese. There are a number of legends and fabled tales regarding the origin of the tea plants. These tales and legends entirely differ from each other. So, these can be the most accepted and relevant arguments regarding the origin of tea plants, which is obscure and a kind of myth. However, the Chinese have enjoyed for originating of tea for the millennia. As per the legend, tea was discovered accidentally by the Chinese King and herbalist Sheh Nung, in 2737 BC (Mitra, 2010). This verse of legend reflects only the discovery of tea, but the origin of the tea plant has not been highlighted. There is another version of the legend on the origin of the tea plants. An Indian religious devotee and prince named Dharma, son of the king Kosjusva, once imposed on himself no sleep during his wonderings. However, he was failed and so grieved. He stretched out his eyes and flung on the ground. It was believed that the tea plant was originated from the eye of Dharma (Samuel, 1882). This verse of argument has been supported by the Japanese and it has been mentioned in their chronicles. In this 21st century, the tale of Dharma may not be acceptable but anyhow Dharma was the first person who introduced the tea plants. However, the actual place of origin of tea is not known. Some scholars believed that the center of origin might be the Tibetan Plateau, including Sze Chuan, Yu-nan, Sain, North East India, or China.

The word 'tea' came from the Chinese Amoy word *t'e*, which is pronounced as *tay*. The Dutch, who were the first to import tea into Europe from the port of Amoy in Fujian Province, called it *thee*, which became 'tea' in English. The Mandarian word for tea is *cha*, became *ch'a* (pronounced as *tcha*) in Cantonese, and in India, it is called *chai*.

Exactly when and how tea spread in China is not known. The Taoist monks and the Buddhists established that consuming tea is a worthy boost for meditation and it is also helpful to enhance the concentration and avoidance of fatigue. The founder of Taoism, Lao-tzu, believed that to excel in meditation, tea is one of the essential ingredients. Tea had become so popular by the 4th century AD that deliberate cultivation of tea became necessary, rather than simply harvesting the leaves from wild bushes. Having started out as an obscure medicinal and religious beverage, tea first seems to have become a domestic drink in China around this time. Tea use was expanded throughout entire China and turned the most popular drink by the Tang dynasty, an era that is regarded as a golden period in Chinese history. Later on, the idea of tea as a beverage travelled gradually from the East to the West by the 16th century.

Genesis of Tea

•   In 2737 BC, tea plant was discovered in China by the Chinese King Shen Nung.

•   In 350 AD for the first time, one of the Chinese dictionaries mentioned tea.

•   In between 400 and 600, the demand for tea increased in China. During that time, tea was consumed as a medicinal beverage. The cultivation process was developed. During this period, the concept of tea was travelled to Japan.

•   In between 648 and 749, Gyoki, the Japanese monk, planted tea in around 50 temple gardens. In Japan, tea was rare and expensive. Only the aristocrats and priests could enjoy it.

•   In 780, tax was first imposed on tea in China.

•   In 1211, Abbot Eisai, a Japanese Buddhist, wrote a book on tea, titled 'Kitcha-Yojoki'.

•   In 1589, Europeans learned about tea.

•   In 1597, the word 'tea' got translated into English for the first time.

•   In 1610, tea was brought by the East India Company. They marketed it as a foreign medical drink. According to them, tea was expensive and common people could not afford it.

•   In 1661, there was a debate on the benefits versus harmful aspects of tea. Dutch doctors were in favor of the health benefits of tea and, on the contrary, German and French doctors highlighted its detrimental aspects.

•   In 1723, the import tax was reduced on tea by Robert Walpole, the British prime minister.

•   In 1765, tea gained popularity in America.

•   In 1778, Joseph Bank, the British naturalist, suggested cultivating tea in India.

- In 1823, indigenous tea was originated in India by Robert Bruce, a Scottish adventurer.
- In 1835, tea cultivation was started in Assam by the East India Company.
- In 1856, tea plantation was started in Darjeeling, India.
- During 1865–67, a situation of tea disaster hit the tea planters in India.
- In 1904, the concept of iced tea was generated by Richard Blechynden.
- In 1909, Thomas Lipton started packaging and blending of tea.
- In 1953, the first instant tea was introduced.

Discovery of Tea Plant in India

In 1823, Robert Bruce, a British soldier and merchant, at the time of his visit to Rangpur, was informed by Singpho Chief, one of the local inhabitants of Northeast India, regarding the existence of indigenous tea plants in Assam. In 1824, Robert Bruce provided some of the plants to CA Bruce, who was the brother of Robert Bruce (Bhuyan, 1974). A few years later, a similar kind of wild plant came to be noticed by Lieutenant Charlton of Assam near Sadiya of Northeast Assam in 1832. Then the wild plant was sent to the Calcutta Botanical Garden.

Tea History in India

The history of the cultivation of tea and the use of tea in India is long back. As per the Indian Ayurveda practice, tea was consumed as tisanes. Indian Ayurveda also revealed that tea leaves were mixed with basil, cardamom, pepper, mint, etc., and consumed to get some medical benefits for maladies (Manoharan, 1974). Later on, the pattern of cultivation and use of tea were changed when the British East India Company arrived in India.

The first record mentioned of tea in India was in 1780, when a few tea bushes from the Canton were planted in Calcutta. These plants did not survive for long, either for want of culture or due to unfavorable weather or soil conditions. These tea bushes were planted for luxury than for any other purpose. The actual emphasis was given in 1788 for the cultivation of tea when Sir J. Bank suggested it. However, the government botanist made a mistake to identify the indigenous tea plant, and due to that, the cultivation of tea was delayed. Later on, Bihar and Cooch Behar were found suitable for tea cultivation. Still then Assam did not come under the regime of the East India Company.

Mr. Scott, the then Governor-General of Assam, in 1819 put effort to cultivate tea on his own in Assam but nothing good was recorded. A few years later, Major Bruce was informed by a Singpho chief of Assam regarding the existence of the indigenous tea plant in Sibsagar region of Assam. Mr. Bruce then informed his brother, CA Bruce. He collected some of the specimens from the jungle of Sibsagar and sent them to D. Scott. D. Scott finally sent those specimens to Dr. Wallich, the botanist. Meanwhile, the monopoly trade of the East India Company between China and Britain was dissolved. At that point of time, the British realized an urgent need for tea cultivation. This was the positive turn for tea in India. However, in 1834, 'Tea committee' was formed under the stewardship of L. W. Bentinck to investigate the possibilities of cultivating tea in India. The committee submitted its report that there were tea plants in many regions of the Northeast frontier. At the same time, Mr. Gordon sent some China varieties of seeds, and these were planted in Calcutta. During his tenure, CA Bruce was appointed as tea forest superintendent in 1836, and he made some remarkable job during his tenure. He set up new tea plantations of China variety at Jaipur, Chauba, and Weenjay; established The Bengal Tea Company at Calcutta; and formed a tea company in London, which were among the major records of his work.

In 1839, for the first time, Indian tea was auctioned in London. A total of eight chests was sold at the auction, and the rates per pound were ranging from 16 shillings to 34 shillings. During 1860–70, tea cultivation spread all over India, but at that tenure, a sizable number of tea gardens faced an unfavorable situation, which has been termed in much literature as 'tea disaster'. However, the disaster did not stay for a longer period. Many gardens were sold at a cheap price and a new company was formed. Thus, the industry turned a steady shift.

Tea History in West Bengal

West Bengal occupies a prestigious position in the Indian tea industry. The overall position of the tea industry of West Bengal is next to Assam. The tea industry of West Bengal is about 165 years old. The commercial tea cultivation was started in 1856. However, before that, the cultivation of tea took place on an experimental basis in 1835. The first experimental tea cultivation was started in West Bengal in the Darjeeling hills when Mr. Garden, a naturalist, returned from China to India. Mr. Garden fetched some tea seeds and seedlings and distributed them in many parts of India for experimental purposes. The same seedlings and seeds were planted in this region. Thus, Dr. Campbell was assigned responsibility for the first experiment in the Darjeeling hills in 1841. He planted those Chinese varieties in Jalpahar and Alubari areas, which were about 7,000-foot elevation. The experiment did not provide any positive results because of unfavorable climatic conditions. Then Mr. Cronemelin set up one of the excremental nurseries in Lebong, located at a lower elevation than the previous excremental area, and succeeded. Afterward, tea cultivation spread across the lower elevation of Darjeeling. However, in 1856, tea cultivation was started commercially. The first tea garden was established in Alubari by the Kurseong and Darjeeling Tea Company. Within 20 years of it, 115 tea gardens were set up, spread over 18,888 acres of land. Meanwhile, tea cultivation was started in the Terai region. The first tea garden, 'Chamta Tea Garden', was established in Terai in 1862 by Mr. J. White. In the succeeding years, Dooars also came to be noticed by the British for tea cultivation. The first tea garden in Dooars was set up by Mr. R. Haughton at Gazaldoba in 1876. Thus, tea cultivation gained popularity in West Bengal. In West Bengal, tea cultivation is mainly confined in the Northern part of it, which is popularly known as North Bengal.

A Brief Sketch of North Bengal

The tea industry of North Bengal lies under the Himalayan foothills and covering the districts of Alipurduar, Jalpaiguri, Darjeeling, and few parts of Coochbehar and North Dinajpur in West Bengal. Technically, the entire tea-producing region of Bengal has been divided into three peripheries: Terai, Dooars, and Darjeeling hills. Terai covers the area of Siliguri sub-division of the Darjeeling district and a part of the North Dinajpur district. The Darjeeling hills cover the Darjeeling sub-division, the Kurseong sub-division, and the Kalimpong sub-division of the Darjeeling district. Dooars entirely covers Jalpaiguri, Alipurduar, and a part of the Coochbehar district. Dooars is the biggest tea-producing region in Bengal and even in North India. A total of 276 organized tea estates (Government of West Bengal, 2014) of the North Bengal play a monumental role in the economy of this region. The industry provides 2,62,426 employments directly and several million indirectly. There are 7 employers' associations and 22 registered trade unions under the banners of different political parties.

Darjeeling

Darjeeling region came to the British regime in the 1800s; before that it was under the Sikkim kingdom. Darjeeling is known as the 'Queen of the Hills'. The name Darjeeling is derived from the Tibetan words 'Dorjee' and 'Ling'—'Dorjee' means thunderbolt and 'Ling' means place. Hence, Darjeeling means the land of thunderbolt.

The entire credit goes to Dr. Campbell, a civil surgeon of British East India Company, for the tea industry of Darjeeling. In 1839, a recommendation was made by the East India Company on the development of tea in Darjeeling. Dr. Campbell was appointed as a consultant for this purpose. Dr. Campbell then started the experiment of the tea plant in 1841. In the first attempt, the experiment failed. After a few years, another botanist, Mr. Cronemelin, got success in his experiment. It took almost 15 years to grow the original plant.

However, based on the result of the experiment, suggestions were made regarding the possibility of tea cultivation in Darjeeling. Later on, the commercial tea plantation was started in 1856. Initially, the China variety of tea was cultivated, but a few years later, the indigenous Assam variety of tea cultivation was started. The first tea garden in Darjeeling was established in 1856 by the Kurseong and Darjeeling Tea company. In 1859, Dhutardia Tea Garden was set up by Dr. Brougham. From 1860 to 1864, more tea gardens were established by the Kurseong and Darjeeling Tea Company in Ambutia, Takdash, Gind, and Phubseing. Lebong Tea Company also expanded to have more number of gardens at Badmatam and Takvar. Several other gardens were established during this period, viz. Makaibari, Steinthal, and Pandam tea estates. There were a total of 39 tea estates, with an approximate area of 10,392 hectares, in 1866. Table 2.1 shows the steady progress of the tea garden in Darjeeling between 1861 and 1951.

Table 2.1 Tea Gardens in Darjeeling (1861–1951)

Year	Number of Gardens	Area Under Cultivation (acres)	Total Approximate Yield in lbs	Average Yield in lbs. per Acre
1861	22	3,251	42,600	13
1866	39	10,392	4,33,715	42
1867	40	9,214	5,82,640	63
1868	44	10,067	8,51,549	85
1869	55	10,769	12,78,869	119
1870	56	11,046	16,89,186	153
1872	74	14,503	29,38,626	203
1873	87	15,695	29,56,710	188
1874	113	18,888	39,27,911	208
1881	155	28,367	51,60,316	182
1885	175	38,495	90,90,500	236
1891	177	45,585	1,09,10,487	239
1895	186	48,692	1,17,14,500	241
1901	170	51,724	1,35,35,537	262
1911	156	51,488	1,42,56,615	277
1921	168	59,005	1,40,80,946	239
1931	169	61,178	2,04,59,481	335
1941	136	63,173	2,48,15,216	393
1951	138	62,580	2,92,83,499	468

Source: Data compiled from Hunter (1972), Dash (1947) and Mitra (1951)

The statistics in the table indicate the rapid progress rate of tea plantations in Darjeeling that took place from 1861 to 1951. Within ten years of
establishment of commercial production of tea in Darjeeling, it has been
observed that 39 tea gardens were opened. The steady improvement of the
tea industry was observed between 1874 and 1895; the area under cultivation improved by 158 percent and the improvement in production was also
observed as 198 percent.

Further, between 1896 and 1901, the number of tea gardens and areas of
cultivation were decreased. The price of tea fell in the international market
and the tea industry was no longer able to earn a profit. Many tea gardens
were merged with another, and some were closed.

Dooars

The lower fertile strip of the base of Bhutan hills is known as Dooars. 'Dooars'
is derived from the Hindusthani word *Dwar*, which means door or gateway. The
logic behind the name Dooars is that the region has at least 18 doors or gateway
to Bhutan. Dooars is the entrance to Bhutan and Northeast India. Dooars has
no political identity; it only has a geographical existence. It is situated over an
area of around 130 kilometers by 50 kilometers. In the west, it stretches from
the river Teesta, and in the east, it stretches from the river Sankosh.

Long back, Dooars was a part of the Coochbehar. In 1661, Coochbehar
was attacked by the Mughals. During the war with Mughals, the king of
Coochbehar realized the need to employ more forces, but within a short
span of period, this was not possible. Then the Konch king asked for help
from Bhutan. Bhutan provided military help to Coochbehar. However,
after the war, the king of Bhutan in lieu of the help wanted the Dooars area
from Coochbehar. Then Coochbehar had no other alternatives and agreed
(Majumder, 1984). Later on, a portion of Dooars, which was known as
Assam Dooars, wrested by the British from the Bhutias in 1837, and the
remaining part of Dooars, i.e., Bengal Dooars, was also wrested by them in
1842 (Hunter, 1877).

Earlier, the Dooars region had two parts: Eastern Dooars and Western
Dooars. The part of Eastern Dooars is now in the Goalpara district of Assam
and its name is no longer known. The Western Dooars, which is regarded
as Dooars of now, was located along with the foothills of Bhutan and the
Sankosh in the east and the Teesta in the west. Dooars is plain land and has
so many streams and deep forests. A sizable portion of land in Dooars is
favorable for the cultivation of paddy, jute, wheat, potato, and other crops.
However, tea is the prime industry of Dooars.

The first tea garden of Dooars opened at Gazaldubi (now it is Gazaldoba). In 1876, Dr. Brougham initiated tea cultivation at Gazaldoba and

took lease 996 acres of land on 16th February 1876. Then, Mr. R. Haugthon was appointed by Dr. Brougham to set up a tea garden at Gazalboda. However, Mr. R. Haugthon is regarded as the pioneer of tea cultivation of Dooars (Ghosh, 1970). Soon after, tea cultivation gained popularity in this region, and within 1877, 22 more tea gardens were opened. Initially, China's variety was cultivated, and later on, Assam and Assam-China hybrid varieties were cultivated.

The tea industry of Dooars has distinct features. The early emergence of entrepreneurship in India was carried out by tea garden owners. Munshi R. Baksh was the first Indian who received a grant for tea cultivation in 1877. The Jaldhaka grant was taken by him on 17 August 1877 and the area was 728 acres. In the same year, Washabari, Dam Dim, Ellenbari, Kumlai, etc., gardens were established. In 1878, more tea gardens continued to be established. Dr. Nilratan Sarkar, the eminent physician of the period, received Kalabari grant. During the same year, Altadanga grant was taken by Kalimohan Roy and Durgabati Sen of 310 acres. However, after a few days, the grant was transferred to Beharilal Ganguly. In 1879, the first Joint Stock Company was formed by the Indians in Jalpaiguri to venture into tea. Thus, by 1930, the total number of estates owned by the Indian entrepreneurs went to 47.

In Table 2.2, the progress of the tea industry in Jalpaiguri is presented:

Table 2.2 Progress of Tea Cultivation in Jalpaiguri (1874–1951)

Year	No. of Gardens	Area (in acres)	Approximate Yield in lbs	Average Yield in lbs per Acre
1874	1	—	—	—
1881	47	5,673	—	—
1891	79	35,683	—	—
1901	235	76,403	31,087,537	407
1911	191	90,85 9	48,820,637	537
1921	131	1,12,688	43,287,187	384
1931	151	1,32,074	66,447,715	503
1941	189	1,31,770	94,604,450	718
1951	158	1,34,473	1,37,194,660	1,020

Source: Data compiled from Biswas (2011) and Mitra (1953)

Terai

Terai, the boggy, and the slender strip of the field are located under the foothills of the Himalayas. The nature of the soil is sandy humus and mixing with boulders. In this region, the suitable climate provides opportunities to grow tea. Terai region is broadly divided into two territories: the Northern Terai and the Southern Terai. The Northern Terai is located in the foothills of the Himalayas and the Southern Terai is located in the plain. The average annual rainfall of this region is around 3,000 millimeters. Terai is composed of the area of the Siliguri sub-division and other plain surroundings of the Darjeeling district. Terai region mainly produced CTC and Orthodox tea (Bhowmik, 1981).

Earlier, Terai was a portion of Sikkim. Terai has a complex history of being a part of the Darjeeling district. Terai was annexed to Darjeeling in 1850. The actual area annexed was around 640 square miles and the lion's portion of it was a dense forest. After a few years, forest lands were converted into cultivation land. Initially, an attempt was made to cultivate paddy. Meanwhile, the cultivation of tea was in full swing in the Darjeeling hills. Tea planters then realized the need to cultivate tea in the available suitable land of Terai. Thus, in 1862, Mr. J. White, who had earlier started tea cultivation in Kurseong, initiated tea cultivation in Champta of Khaprial in Terai. By then, tea cultivation was started in Terai, and in the following years, tea cultivation spread across the entire Terai region from the north to the south.

References

Baildon, S. (1882). *The tea industry in India*. London, England: W. H. Allen, p. 13.

Bhowmik, S. K. (1981). *Class formation in the plantation system*. New Delhi, India: Peoples Publishing House, p. 2.

Bhuyan, S. K. (1974). *Anglo-Assamese relations, 1771–1826: A history of the relations of Assam with the East India Company from 1771 to 1826, based on original English and Assamese sources*. Guwahati, India: Lawyer's Book Stall, p. 26.

Biswas, D. (2011). *Productivity and industrial relations: An empirical study on tea estates in Dooars region of West Bengal* (Unpublished doctoral thesis). University of North Bengal, Darjeeling, India.

Dash, A. J. (1947). *Bengal district gazetteers-Darjeeling*. Alipore, India: Bengal Government Press, p. 114.

Ghosh, B. C. (1970). The development of the tea industry in the district of Jalpaiguri 1869–1968. In Charuchandra Sanyal et al. (Eds.), *Jalpaiguri district centenary souvenir* (p. 283). Calcutta, India: Newman's Printers.

Government of India. (1951). *Census of India: West Bengal, Sikkim and Chandernagore, Part II-Tables*, A. K. Mitra. Delhi, India: Manager Publications, p. 266.

Government of West Bengal. (2014). *Synopsis on survey of tea gardens*. Kolkata, India: Joint Labour Commissioner, North Bengal Zone, p. 5.

Hunter, W. W. (1877). *Statistical account of Bengal. Vol. XX*. London, England: Trubner & Co., pp. 219–220.

Hunter, W. W. (1972). *A statistical account of Bengal. Vol. X* (Reprint in India). Delhi, India: D. K. Publication House, p. 165.

Majumder, A. B. (1984). *Britain and the Kingdom of Bhutan*. Patna, India: Bharati Bhavan, p. 18.

Manoharan, S. (1974). *Indian tea, a strategy for development*. New Delhi, India: S. Chand & Co Pvt. Limited, p. 55.

Mitra, A. K. (1953). *Census of India 1951, Vol. VI, Part 1A (West Bengal, Sikkim and Chandernagore)*. Alipore, India: Bengal Government Press, p. 266.

Mitra, D. (2010). *Globalization and industrial relations in tea plantations*. New Delhi, India: Abhijit Publications, p. 13.

3 Growth and Development of Tea Industry in India

Particularly in North Bengal

The Growth of the Indian Tea Industry

The growth of the Indian tea industry may be distinguished based on the two major periods:

i. The period before the five-year plans (1850–1950), and
ii. The five-year plans period (1951 to the succeeding years).

I. THE PERIOD BEFORE THE FIVE-YEAR PLANS (1850–1950)

Tea cultivation began in India in 1834 on an experimental basis. The commercial cultivation of tea was started in 1839 after the establishment of the Assam Tea Company. In the following year, several companies were established and the rate of growth was found remarkable. Form the year 1850, the industry took a sharp turn. Within the 40 years of it, the unbelievable growth was recorded in all aspects, such as areas of production, total production, and average yield per hectare of the tea industry. On the other hand, the period 1890–1918 witnessed an overall development of the tea industry (Shown in Table 3.1). The following are the factors that were responsible for the growth of the industry:

a) During this tenure, the cultivation of tea in South India took shape as an industry. The notable development of this tenure is the formation of the United Planters Association of South India (UPASI) and many other employers' association in North India;
b) The emphasis was given on the research and development of tea cultivations;
c) Enactment of Indian Tea Act, 1903;
d) Development activities were initiated to set up railway tracks in North India.

Table 3.1 Growth of the Tea Industry in India (During 1850–1950)

Year	Area Under Cultivation (Thousand Hectare)	Production (Million Kilogram)	Yield Per Hectare (in Kilogram)
1850	0.75	0.097	130
1890	152	57	373
1918	275	173	629
1939	337	205	610
1950	316	278	881

Source: Combination of various statistics of Tea Board of India.

From 1918 to 1939, the Indian tea industry passed a period of turmoil. Hence, no significant growth was observed in this tenure. From 1919 to 1920, a drastic fall in the price of tea was observed; production was also decreased significantly in 1921. In 1929, the global depression badly impacted the tea industry. Consequently, the tea industry became non-remunerative due to a decline in consumption as a result of the global recession.

Between 1939 and 1950, the tea industry of India got oxygen after a long period for World War II. During the war, tea production was stopped in some countries like Indonesia, Malaysia, Sri-Lanka, etc. Indian tea companies grasped this opportunity and exported a huge quantity of tea in the global market. Ultimately, the Indian tea industry earned huge revenue. This was the strategic turning point for the Indian tea industry. During that time, the UK government became the buyer of Indian tea. Thus, the profitability of the industry improved gradually. Enactment of the Central Tea Board Act, 1949, was one of the customized initiatives for the industry. Yet, the North Indian tea industry faced a stiff shortage of manpower during the war.

II. THE FIVE-YEAR PLAN PERIOD (1951 ONWARD)

The Government of India appointed a committee during the first planning period in 1952 under the supervision of Rajaram Rao. The committee was named as 'Rajaram Rao Committee on Tea'. However, the committee was formed to trace out the difficulties confronted by the tea industry. Accordingly, the committee provided suggestions to revamp the industry. Reduction of central excise duty, finance from the bank, relaxation of income tax, etc., were some of those suggestions provided by the committee. Tea Act, 1953, was constituted in this plan period. Tea Board of India was set up under the Tea Act, 1953, during this tenure.

The second plan period had negative and positive impacts on the tea industry. The negative impact was the creation of the Suez channel in 1956. The Suez issues made Indian tea trade difficult with its largest buyer, the UK. On the other hand, the positive role was played by the Plantation Enquiry Commission. In this planning period, the commission recommended on vital issues. The issues were cost reduction, financial assistance for the tea industry, re-plantation program, export promotion, etc.

We observed the overall development of the Indian tea industry during the third plan period. During this tenure, several tea auction centers were opened. The railway transportation was arranged for the transportation of tea and coal.

During the fourth plan period, the Guwahati auction center was established. It was the first auction center in Assam. In 1970, the Indian Tea Association appointed a special committee. Mr. M. Lamond was the chairman of this committee. The committee was formed to accelerate the improvement of tea production. Foreign Exchange Regulation Act, 1973, was also enacted in this period.

The fifth plan period witnessed a glorious turn of the Indian tea industry. The unpredicted and abnormal price was raised in all auction centers in pan India and even in the foreign market. In this period, the Siliguri auction center was established. In 1978, the 'Tea Marketing Committee' was formed. Mr. P. Tandon was the chairman of this committee.

The important event of the sixth plan period was the national-level meets of the representative of all tea-producing states. This was the first time that due importance was given to the small growers of the country. The outcomes of this meets were: (a) the priority area—export and quality were highlighted; (b) reduction of excise duty and indirect tax on export, etc.

The tea industry initiated several activities during the seventh plan period. The initiatives were purely related to the tea plantation. During this period, West Bengal Tea Development Corporation was modernized. Darjeeling tea logo was launched in this plan period.

During the eight five-year plan period, the tea industry was badly affected due to the liberalization, privatization, and globalization policy. During the entire period, the tea industry experienced unstable prices in its auction market. The average auction price of tea was declined in 1992 and the price was again increased in 1993. Again in 1994, the price was declined in the auction market. The quantity of production of tea was downturned in 1992. In the ninth plan period, production increased very negligibly, around 0.4 percent. The export scenario remained the same during the ninth plan period. In terms of the monetary value of the export, an improvement was observed because the unit value of export was raised from Rs. 85.79 to Rs. 87.13 per kilogram of tea. In the tenth plan tenure, the export of tea declined to 184 million kilograms. In the following (Table 3.2), a detail account of description of the Indian tea industry has been presented in terms of area, production, yield, and export for the period of 1990 to 2016.

Table 3.2 Scenario of Indian Tea Industry During Post-Globalization Period (Based on 1990)

Year	Area (hectare)	Production (th. kg)	Yield (kg/ hectare)	Export Qty. (th./ kg)
1990	4,16,269	7,20,338	1,730	2,10,024
1995	4,27,065	7,56,016	1,770	1,67,996
2000	5,04,366	8,46,922	1,679	2,06,816
2005	5,55,611	9,45,974	1,703	1,99,050
2006	5,67,020	9,81,805	1,732	2,18,737
2007	5,78,458	9,86,427	1,705	1,78,754
2008	5,79,353	9,80,818	1,693	2,03,117
2009	5,79,353	9,79,000	1,689	1,97,903
2010	5,79,353	9,66,400	1,668	2,22,019
2011	5,79,353	1,115,720	1,925	2,15,410
2012	5,63,979	1,126,330	1,997	2,08,230
2013	5,63,979	1,200,040	2,127	2,19,060
2014	5,63,979	1,207,310	2,141	2,07,440
2015	5,66,660	1,208,660	2,133	2,28,660
2016	5,66,660	1,267,360	2,236	2,22,450

Source: Combination of various statistics of Tea Board of India and Indian Tea Association.

In the 11th five-year plan period, the financial health of the tea industry was not good. The tea industry especially in the West Bengal region was in deep crisis. Several tea estates were closed or abandoned in this tenure. Dooars and the Terai region of the Indian tea industry were in the news headlines over the years. The socio-economic foundation of the entire tea-producing region of North Bengal was severely affected. Thousands of tea labors and their family members died during this period only because of malnutrition and starvation. On the eve of the 12th five-year plan period, the situation remained the same.

Major Tea-Growing Regions in India

In India, the entire tea-growing region is broadly classified into two categories: the North Indian tea industry and South Indian tea industry. These regions are spread all over India, some of which are world famous. Generally, tea plantations are located in backward areas of rural hills in India (Griffiths, 1967). Major tea-growing areas in India are located in West Bengal, Assam, Karnataka, Kerala, and Tamil Nadu. Beyond these, there are other locations where tea is grown in small quantities; these areas are Arunachal Pradesh, Tripura, Himachal Pradesh, Sikkim, Uttaranchal, Nagaland, Manipur, Mizoram, Meghalaya, Bihar, and Orissa (Hazarika, 2011).

Growth and Development of Tea Industry in West Bengal

Earlier we have discussed the history of tea cultivation in West Bengal. In this section, the focus is on the growth and development of the tea industry in West Bengal. Further, discussions have been made on each tea-growing area of West Bengal. The growth and development patterns have been discussed on the basis of the production of tea, the area under cultivation of tea, and the number of tea gardens.

It is observed from Table 3.3 that the tea production in West Bengal has raised by 299.31 percent over the last 63 years tenure—i.e., from 1951 to 2014. The table also depicts the growth rate of tea production in the entire three regions of West Bengal. The highest rate of growth is observed in the Terai region (1865.80 percent) followed by the Dooars region (177.91 percent), and the Darjeeling region (13.66 percent) during the last 63 years.

Figure 3.1 shows that the comparative scenario of tea production among the three tea-producing belts of West Bengal. In West Bengal, among the three tea-producing belts, Dooars is in the topmost position in terms of production of tea, followed by Terai, and Darjeeling. It is also noticed from the figure that the Terai region has turned toward upward of tea production in the year 1990 and has been producing in the same rhythm till 2014. On the other side, from the same year, the Darjeeling region has found a downturn in tea production. However, in the case of Dooars, it is noticed that in 2001 the production of tea has turned more upward.

It is observed from Table 3.4 that the area under cultivation of tea in West Bengal has also raised by 76.46 percent over the last 63 years tenure, i.e., from 1951 to 2014. The table also depicts the growth rate of the areas of tea cultivation in the entire three regions in West Bengal. The highest rate of growth in terms of area of tea cultivation land is observed in the Terai region (189.91 percent) followed by the Dooars region (33.52 percent), and the Darjeeling region (7.55 percent) over the last 63 years.

Figure 3.2 shows the comparative scenario of the tea cultivation area among the three tea-producing belts of West Bengal. According to the figure, the Dooars region has the maximum tea plantation area followed by the Terai and Darjeeling. The figure also depicts that the tea cultivation area of the Terai region has increased unpredictably from 2000 onward. On the

Table 3.3 Production of Tea in Three Regions of West Bengal (Figures in '000 kg)

Region / State	1951	1961	1971	1981	1990	2001	2014	% Increase over 1951
Darjeeling	7,839	10,107	10,293	12,226	14,499	9,841	8,910	13.66
Terai	6,376	9,253	12,954	15,782	21,130	49,388	1,25,340	1,865.80
Dooars	63,994	66,898	80,840	1,00,251	1,14,124	1,27,611	1,77,850	177.91
West Bengal	78,158	86,258	1,04,087	1,28,259	1,49,735	1,86,840	3,12,100	299.31

Source: Combination of various statistics of Tea Board of India and Indian Tea Association.

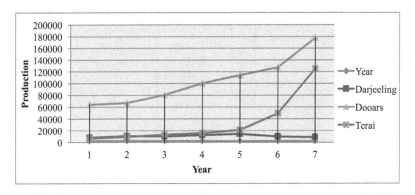

Figure 3.1 Comparative Scenario of Tea Production Among Three Regions in West Bengal

Source: Author's own calculation.

Table 3.4 Area of Cultivation of Tea in Three Regions of West Bengal (Figure in Hectares)

Region / State	1951	1961	1971	1981	1990	2000	2014	% Increase over 1951
Darjeeling	16,569	18,605	18,245	19,239	20,065	17,228	17,820	7.55
Dooars	54,609	54,756	59,485	63,418	67,760	69,703	72,920	33.52
Terai	8,402	9,344	10,769	11,314	13,345	20,548	49,700	189.91
West Bengal	79,580	82,705	88,499	93,971	1,01,170	1,07,479	1,40,440	76.47

Source: Combination of various statistics of Tea Board of India and Indian Tea Association.

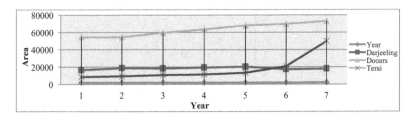

Figure 3.2 Scenario of Tea Cultivation Area Among Three Regions in West Bengal

Source: Author's own calculation.

other hand, the tea cultivation area of the Darjeeling region has decreased from 1990 onward.

Darjeeling

In Darjeeling, the cultivation of tea dated back to 1835 on a trial basis. Commercial cultivation was started in 1856. The Kurseong and Darjeeling Tea Company were the first organized tea company in Darjeeling to set up tea estates. Within five years of starting the commercial cultivation of tea in Darjeeling, the number of tea garden was increased to 22.

Number of Tea Gardens in Darjeeling

The growth of the number of the tea garden in Darjeeling hills is presented in Table 3.5(Between 1961 and 2014):

Table 3.5 Growth of Number of Tea Gardens in Darjeeling (1961–2014)

Year	Number of Tea Gardens	Year	Number of Tea Gardens
1961	99	1995	83
1980	103	2000	85
1985	102	2005	85
1990	102	2014	81

Source: Combination of various statistics of Tea Board of India.

Table 3.5 shows that the number of tea gardens decreased from 102 to 83 during the period 1990–1995, i.e., which is around 19 percent. Since, we understood that the year 1991 as the starting of a new economic policy that advocated the doctrine of LPG (liberalization, privatization, and globalization) policy. The new economic policy might cause a decline in the number of tea gardens in the Darjeeling hills. In the subsequent years, it was noticed that the number of tea estates had been increased but again in 2014 the number has gone down. Although, the percentage of increase and decrease in the number of tea gardens between 1995 and 2014 is very negligible. However, the new economic policy impacted on the tea industry of Darjeeling.

Production of Tea in Darjeeling

The statistics in Table 3.6 of tea production of Darjeeling reveal that over 63 years, the production of tea has increased by 13.66 percent. The decade of 1951–1961 observed the maximum percent increase of production of

Table 3.6 Production of Tea in Darjeeling (Figures in '000 kg)

Year	1951	1961	1971	1981	1990	2001	2014	% increase over 1951
Production	7,839	10,107	10,293	12,226	14,499	9,841	8,910	13.66

Source: Combination of various statics of Tea Board of India.

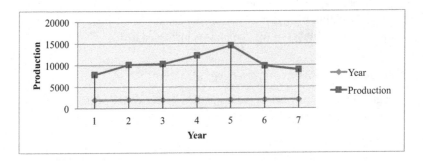

Figure 3.3 Trend of Tea Production in Darjeeling
Source: Author's own calculation.

tea, which is 28.93 percent. On the other side, the decade from 1990 to 2001 observed the maximum percent decrease of production of tea, which is about 32.12 percent. However, the sharp fall of tea production during the period of 1990–2001 indicates that globalization has a negative impact of the tea production of this region. Because, in the year 1991, the LPG policy was conceived, and the negative impact of it continued to the subsequent years.

Figure 3.3 of the production of tea in the Darjeeling region is legible that the sharp fall of tea production from 1990 onward. It is also noticed that from 1951 onward the trend of tea production was upward till 1990, but particularly after this point of time, the downward trend of tea production is observed.

Area of Tea Cultivation in Darjeeling

It has been noticed that the area under tea cultivation in Darjeeling rose by 7.55 percent over 63 years (1951–2014).

The cultivation area of tea in Darjeeling is found maximum growth in between 1951 and 1961. The growth in between these particular periods is observed 12.28 percent, followed by the period of 1971–1981 (5.49 percent), and 2000–2014 (3.43 percent). In the following figure, the growth pattern of the area under tea cultivation in Darjeeling is observed.

Further, it has been observed that the area of tea cultivation in Darjeeling has reduced from 1990 onward. This indicates that due to globalization, many tea companies stopped their operations in Darjeeling. This also confirmed that globalization had a worse impact on the tea industry in Darjeeling.

Dooars Region

In 1874, Mr. R. Haughton started the cultivation of tea in Gazaldubi (now it is Gajaldoba) of Dooars (Saha and Ghosh, 2013). This was the first tea garden in Dooars. Mr. R. Haughton is regarded as the pioneer of the tea industry of Dooars (Ghosh, 1970). After the setup of the first tea garden in Dooars, the cultivation of tea was started randomly.

Number of Tea Gardens in Dooars

In 1876, 13 tea gardens had been established. However, the growth of the number of tea garden in the Dooars region is presented in Table 3.7.

The table shows that from 1876 to 1901, the number of gardens was increased rapidly. On the contrary, after 1991 onward, the number was decreased gradually. Between 1892 and 1901, it is noticed that the maximum number of tea gardens was increased. Actually, during this period the highest number of grants (area of land offered on lease for tea plantation by the government) was provided. There were many grants in the Jalpaiguri district, and the number of tea gardens in 1901 represents the number of grants. The actual number of tea garden was fewer than 235.

Table 3.7 Growth of Number of Tea Gardens in Dooars (1876–2014)

Year	Number of Tea Gardens	Year	Number of Tea Gardens
1876	13	1941	189
1881	55	1951	158
1892	182	1961	155
1901	235	1971	151
1921	131	1990	163
1931	151	2014	150

Source: Combination of Tea Board of India, Labour Department of Government of West Bengal, and Griffith (1967).

Production of Tea in Dooars

Table 3.8 reveals that the tea production of Dooars was increasing since 1951. The statistics of tea production indicate that over the past decades, the tea industry of Dooars has performed excellently. In 2000–2014, the tea production was observed maximum than the other decades, which was 39.36 percent. From the period of 1990–2001, the least quantity of tea was produced in Dooars. This least quantity of production evidence that the ill effect of globalization on the tea industry.

Figure 3.4 reflects the growth trends of tea production in Dooars from 1961 to 2014. Over the last 63 years, tea production of Dooars has been raised to 177.91 percent. The growth of production was observed as 4.53 percent during 1951–1961, 20.84 percent during 1961–1971, 24.01 percent during 1971–1981, 13.83 percent during 1981–1990, 11.81 percent during 1990–2000, and 39.36 percent during 2000–2014.

Area of Tea Cultivation in Dooars

It has been noticed that areas of tea cultivation in Dooars have been increased by 33.53 percent over 63 years. The period from 1961 to 1971 has been observed as the maximum increase in the area of tea cultivation in this region.

Table 3.8 Production of Tea in Dooars (Figures in '000 kg)

Year	1951	1961	[1971	1981	1990	2001	2014	% Increase over 1951
Production	63,994	66,898	80,840	1,00,251	1,14,124	1,27,611	1,77,850	177.91

Source: Combination of various statistics of Tea Board of India.

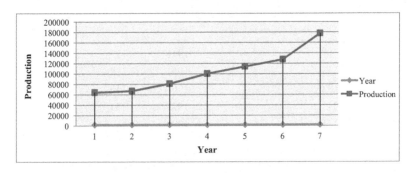

Figure 3.4 Trend of Tea Production in Dooars

Source: Author's own calculation.

Further, it is noticed that the growth of the cultivation area during the period of 1951–1961 was very negligible, only 0.26 percent; otherwise, almost in every period, satisfactory growth was observed. However, from 1990 to 2000, the growth of the tea cultivation area was found to be only 2.86 percent.

Terai

The whole credit goes to Mr. J. White for initiating tea cultivation in the Terai region. Terai was equipped with its first tea garden at Champta, close to Siliguri, in 1862. However, the industry developed afterward. The growth of the number of tea gardens in the Terai region is presented in Table 3.9.

Number of Tea Gardens in Terai

From the table, it is noticed that from 1961 to 1990, the number of tea gardens was increasing systematically. From 1990 onward, it took a downturn. The sudden decrease in the number of tea gardens from the year 1990 indicates the worse effects of globalization. However, no uniform statistics are available regarding the number of tea estates in the West Bengal region. The published statistics by the various organizations on the number of tea estates in West Bengal are not the same. Hence, this is a matter of confusion.

Growth of Tea Production in Terai

Table 3.10 reveals that the production of tea cultivation has increased by 1,865.80 percent over 63 years, i.e., from 1951 to 2014. Tea production of the Terai region recorded a steady progress over the last six decades.

Table 3.9 Growth of Number of Tea Gardens in Terai (1961–2014)

Year	Number of Tea Gardens	Year	Number of Tea Gardens
1961	47	1986	62
1971	48	1988	73
1980	48	1990	82
1985	63	2014	45

Source: Combination data from Mitra (2010), Government of West Bengal (2013).

Table 3.10 Production of Tea in Terai (Figures in '000 kg)

Year	1951	1961	1971	1981	1990	2001	2014	% Increase over 1951
Production	**6,376**	**9,253**	**12,954**	**15,782**	**21,130**	**49,388**	**1,25,340**	**1865.80**

Source: Statistics of Tea Board of India.

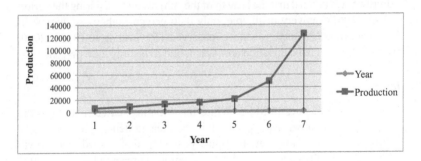

Figure 3.5 Trend of Tea Production in Terai
Source: Authors own calculation.

Figure 3.5 of tea production in the Terai region shows a positive trend since 1951. The maximum production of tea has been observed during 2001–2014, which is 153 percent followed by the period during 1990 to 2001 (133.73 percent), 1951–1961 (45.12 percent), 1961–1971 (39.99 percent), 1981–1990 (33.88 percent), and 1971–1981 (21.83 percent). While the performances of the other tea-producing regions were passive during 1990–2014, Terai region has shown an outstanding performance.

Tea Cultivation Area in Terai

It is noticed that the area of tea cultivation in Terai has been increased by 491.52 percent for 63 years, i.e., in 1951–2014. From 1990 onwards, it took a sharp upward turn. However, the period 2001–2014 has shown the maximum increase in the area of tea cultivation in this region, which was 141.87 percent.

Particulars of Employer/Management Associations

There is seven tea planters' association/management in the North Bengal region of the Indian tea industry. These are as follows:

  i. Dooars Branch of Indian Tea Association (DBITA)
 ii. Terai Branch of Indian Tea Association (TBITA)
iii. Darjeeling Tea Association (DTA)
 iv. Darjeeling Branch of Indian Tea Association (DITA)
  v. Indian Tea Planters Association (ITPA)
 vi. Tea Association of India (TAI)
vii. Terai Indian Planters' Association (TIPA)

In the tea industry of North Bengal, DBITA is the largest employers' association, having membership of 94 tea estates followed by DTA, ITPA, TAI, DITA, and TIPA. Eleven tea estates do not belong to any employer association.

References

Ghosh, B. C. (1970). *Development of the tea industry in the district of Jalpaiguri 1869–1968*. Calcutta, India: Newman's Printers, p. 23.

Government of West Bengal. (2013). *Synopsis on survey of tea gardens*. Kolkata, India: State Labour Institute, WB, p. 5.

Griffiths, P. (1967). *The history of the Indian tea industry*. London, England: Weidenfeld and Nicolson, pp. 89–92.

Hazarika, K. (2011). Changing market scenario for Indian tea. *International Journal of Trade, Economics and Finance*, 2(4), pp. 285–287.

Mitra, D. (2010). *Globalization and industrial relations in tea plantations*. New Delhi, India: Abhijit Publications.

Saha, S. P., and Ghosh, A. G. (2013). *Development of the tea industry in the district of Jalpaiguri 1869–1968*. In B. C. Ghosh (Ed.), *Development of the tea industry in the district of Jalpaiguri 1869–1968* (p. 10). Siliguri, India: N. L. Publishers.

4 Span of Management and Procurement Practices in Tea Estates of North Bengal

Organizational Structure of a Typical Tea Estate

The organizational hierarchy is generally rigid in the tea plantation industry in India. The typical organizational structure in tea plantation can be alienated into five parts; the owner, manager, staff (*Babu*), sub-staff (*sardar*), and labor. However, in the following (Figure 4.1) typical organizational structure has been presented.

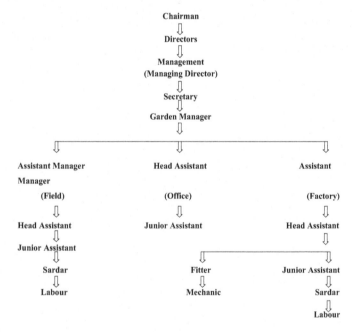

Figure 4.1 Typical Organizational Structure of a Tea Estate
Source: Author's Own Creation.

Generally, in tea plantations, the general manager has control over the factory manager and plantation manager. One or more assistant or junior managers perform their works under the supervision of the factory manager. Similarly, in the case of the plantation (field), one or more assistant or junior managers are supervised by the field manager. The manager of any tea plantation is acknowledged as *Bara Saheb* and the assistant managers are popularly called as *Chota Saheb*. There is a group of staff among the workers to assist the assistant managers, who are commonly referred to as *Babu*. Generally, they are the senior staff of the plantation industry. The clerical employees in tea plantation are regarded as staff, and supervisors in the field/factory, watchman, etc., are regarded as sub-staff. This class of staff workers is promoted directly from the labor (Mitra, 2012). In tea plantations, the social difference between worker and manager is maintained in a disciplined manner.

Span of Management

The span of management refers to the number of subordinates a superior has under his direct supervision. V. A. Graicunas, a French management counselor, philosopher, and an engineer, in the year 1933, published a paper on 'Relationship in Organization' and mentioned that three key types of relationships exist between superior and subordinates (Urwick, 1956). These are:

  i. Direct single relationships,
 ii. Direct group relationships, and
iii. Cross relationships.

The relationship increases manifold if the number of subordinates is increased gradually. If the number of the subordinate is one, then the relationships will be. If it is two, the relationship will be 6, and so on. He explained such a relationship with a wonderful scientific formula. The formula is presented here:

$$r = n\left[2^{n}\!\!/_{2} + (n-1)\right]$$

Here, r = number of relationships that will be calculated, n = number of subordinates that are given.

If we calculate by using this formula, then the following number of relationships will be created (Table 4.1).

Table 4.1 Graicunas Relationship of Supervisor and Subordinate

Number of subordinates	Number of relationships
1	1
2	6
3	18
4	44
5	100
6	244

Source: Author's own calculation based on the formula.

Example of Graicunas control relationship:

Assume that, Tatan (T) is superior; Joy (J) and Arup (A) are his subordinates. As per Graicunas, T has to control over the following relations:

i.   **Direct Individual Relations:** T with J and T with A. Here, two direct relations have been observed.
ii. **Group Relations:** T with J in the presence of A, T with A in the presence of J. Here, also two such group relations have been observed.
iii. **Cross Relations:** J with A and A with J, i.e., again two relations have been observed.

Hence, T has to control total (2+2+2) = 6 relationships.

By using this formula, we can easily calculate the number of relationships that exist between superiors and subordinates. Graicunas has argued that for a superior it is very difficult to control a large number of subordinates because of the complexity in the relationship. It is very difficult to control more than five or in some cases six subordinates at a time (Urwick, 1938).

Accepting the Graicunas formula for the span of management a standard, the scenario of the span of management in tea plantations of the North Bengal region is extremely poor. In Table 4.2, a detailed account of the span of management in tea plantations of North Bengal has been presented.

Table 4.2 exhibits the supervisor and subordinates' ratio in the tea plantations of North Bengal. In Public Limited Tea Company, the ratio is 1:37, for

Table 4.2 Average of Supervisor Versus Workers Ratio in the Tea Plantations of North Bengal Region

SL No.	Types of Plantation	Supervisor Vs. Workers Ratio
1.	Public Limited Tea Company	1:37
2.	Proprietorship Tea Company	1:85
3.	Partnership Tea Company	1:42
4.	Public Sector Undertakings Tea Company	1:71

Source: Field survey, 2017

Proprietorship Tea Company, it is 1:85; for Partnership Tea Company, it is 1:42;, and for Public Sector Undertakings Tea Company, the ratio is 1:71. This is clear from the supervisor-verses-subordinates ratios of various types of tea plantations in this region. The quality control over subordinates is not up to the standard. The standard of the span of control as suggested by the experts' stands to be 1:6; in the tea plantations in North Bengal, it is found to be ranging between 1:37 and 1:85. Thus, it may be concluded that the span of control over subordinates is very poor in the region.

Composition of Human Resources in the Tea Industry of North Bengal

However, a brief highlight in respect of the composition of human resources in the tea industry of North Bengal (based on the report of Labour Department, Government of West Bengal, 2013) has been presented below:

I. WORKMEN

a) **Daily Rated Workers:**

There are a total of 2,18,968 daily rated workers in the Tea Estates of Hill, Terai, and Dooars.

b) **Casual (Bigha) Workers:**

A total of 67,440 Casual (*Bigha*) workers were engaged by the Tea Estates of Hill, Terai, and Dooars during 2012.

c) **Staff/ Sub-Staff/ Workers in Factory:**

A total of 15,362 workmen, including staff and sub-staff, have been engaged in 235 factories of tea estates. Out of these factories, 38 tea estates have not engaged any worker in the factory.

d) Contract Labor:

A total of 2,892 contract laborers have been engaged by only 20 tea estates. The remaining tea estates have not yet engaged in any contract labor.

e) Nayaginti Workers:

As per the tripartite industry-wise settlement of 1999 'Nayaginti Workers' (5778) have been engaged by 158 tea estates. Out of these tea estates, 115 tea estates are yet to engage 'Nayaginti Workers'.

f) Bastiyar Labor:

A total of 8,522 bastiyar laborers have been engaged only in 31 tea estates.

g) Computer Operator:

A total of 250 computer operators have been engaged by 143 tea estates.

h) Sub-Staff (OMRE):

There are 16,347 sub-staffs (OMRE) engaged by 269 tea estates of Hill, Terai, and Dooars region.

i) Sub-Staff (Medical):

There are 564 sub-staffs (medical) who have been engaged by 132 tea estates.

j) Staff (Clerical/ Technical):

There are 4,775 staffs (clerical/ technical) who have been engaged by 267 tea estates of Hill, Terai, and Dooars region.

h) Staff (Medical):

There are 400 staffs (Medical) who have been engaged by 175 tea estates of Hill, Terai, and Dooars region.

II.   MANAGERIAL PERSONNEL

Generally, tea estates are run by experienced managerial executives. They are responsible for the smooth and efficient functioning of tea estates to maintain desired development, industrial peace, and harmony. Details of the composition of the managerial executives have been presented in this section based on the field survey.

- Changmari tea estate has the highest number, i.e., 23 managerial executives.
- 36 tea estates have engaged ten or more managerial executives.
- 146 tea estates have engaged five to nine managerial executives.
- 90 tea estates have engaged two to four managerial executives.
- 7 tea estates mainly depend on a single manager.

III. PROFESSIONAL QUALIFICATIONS OF MANAGERIAL PERSONNEL

A total of 188 tea estates have managers who are simply graduate and having no professional or technical diploma/degree relating to tea. The managers of 35 tea estates are simply postgraduate without any professional or technical background. There are only 53 managers who have professional/ technical background, i.e., degree/ diploma to manage the tea estate.

IV. LABOR WELFARE OFFICERS

- There is no labor welfare officer in 175 tea estates.
- Each of 12 tea estates has 2 labor welfare officers.
- Each of 86 tea estates has only one labor welfare officer.
- 79 tea estates have labor welfare officers who have a professional qualification.
- 55 labor welfare officers have passed the viva voce test of Labour Department.
- 24 labor welfare officers have applied or appeared in viva voce test of Labour Department.

Procurement Function in Tea Plantation of Bengal

Labor Recruitment

Recruitment is one of the essential steps in the procurement process of the management of human resources. The success of the business fundamentally depends on the temperament of human resources deployed. The tea industry is exclusively labor dependent. Suitable nurturing of tea plants is extremely important throughout the year. From the preparation of nursery soil for rooting to the packaging of tea for sale, a huge number of laborers are required throughout the year. Every job has its specifications which call for a specialized workforce in this sector. For the plucking purpose, women workers are regarded as the most suitable. At the time of plucking the leaves, due concentration is given to the young tea bushes. Due to the distinct configuration of fingers, women workers are given preference in comparison to male workers in the jobs of plucking and sorting. Likewise, for spraying of chemicals, manure, and most of the factory works, male workers are usually preferred.

At the outset of the tea industry in India, tea planters confronted with difficulties while recruiting labor. Tea plantations were located in distant and unpopulated areas of the hilly regions surrounded by jungles and unhealthy climates. The surrounding areas of the tea plantations were inhabited by tigers, snakes, and other such wild animals. The regions were also engulfed by deadly diseases like Kala-Jar, malaria, etc. (Ghosh, 1970). Under such conditions, labor recruitment from the adjoining areas was too difficult for the planters.

The migration of the labor toward the tea plantations in North Bengal started during the mid-1950s of the 19th century. With the expansion of tea plantations, the demand for laborers increased. During that period, the plantation management had to depend upon the contractors who procured labor to the tea plantations (Barua, 2008). However, this system of labor recruitment was entirely abolished in 1915. In 1917, all labor contractors amalgamated themselves and formed Tea District Labour Associations (TDLA). Afterward, the TDLA was actively entrusted with the task of procurement of labor from the different regions for the tea gardens. Initially, labor was recruited on a family basis. Labor was recruited from the tribal areas of Chotanagpur plateau (Sarkar, 1992). Usually, labor was recruited for the short term. As per the terms of the agreement, labors were required to go back to their native places. The provision of 'Repatriation Allowance' was prevalent for the repatriated workers. However, the labor and their families never returned to their respective natives with repatriation allowances after the terminations of their agreement. Thus, the existing labors settled in the tea plantations permanently, and gradually new labor recruitment was stopped.

Labor Recruitment Practice in the Tea Industry of North Bengal

However, the history of the recruitment of labor force in the tea industry of the North Bengal region is very long and is quite conventional. The tea laborers were recruited from the descendants of the migrants coming from different parts of the country and sometimes outside the country also. In the beginning, the tea industry failed to attract local people due to the hazardous work conditions and abysmally low rate of wages. These issues compelled the management of tea plantations to recruit labor from distant places through different sources. Tea workers of the North Bengal (except Darjeeling hills) were the actual residents of the tribal region of Chotanagpur plateau. In the tea industry of Darjeeling, nearly the entire workforce comprised the migrants from Nepal.

LABOR RECRUITMENT PRACTICE IN DOOARS AND TERAI

In 1876, while the tea plantation industry was in the early stage, the region of Dooars had a very small population. Local people had sufficient land to survive. They did not agree to work in the tea plantations. So, planters were adopted from other sources of recruitment of labor.

Mainly two types of recruitment system prevailed in the tea industry of Dooars and Terai region: through *Sardar* (Government of India Report, 1966) and *Arkati*. *Sardars* were the settled migrated staff members of tea plantations. *Arkatis*, on the other hand, were the Bengali educated staffs (known as *Babu*) and were recruited from the adjoining areas. *Sardars* went to the tribal areas to lure the *Adivasi* people to work in the tea gardens. Chotanagpur plateau served as the main catchment area for labor recruitment. The *Adivasis* were attracted by the *Sardars* with every prospect and advantage for their family. Sometimes, poverty-stricken migrant workers were offered loans by the *Sardars* of tea gardens. The amount of loan was used to pay debts of poor peasants, ruined artisans, and agricultural laborers to the *Zamindars* (landlord). The *Sardar* who fetched them and recruited them in the garden work was entitled to receive a commission. This kind of system was prevalent in the tea gardens run by the British.

Another type of recruitment practice was also prevalent mostly in private tea gardens. In private tea gardens, laborers were recruited through private agencies. Garden management sent their representatives, known as *Arkati*, to the recruitment area. The *Arkatis* had tied up with some local persons or agencies in the recruitment area. The *Arkati* used to propose the number of labor requirements to the agencies, and the agencies in turn supplied the required labor to the respective tea gardens. These agencies were paid by the garden. This kind of labor recruitment practice was known as Grimatias (Rage, 1946).

LABOR RECRUITMENT PRACTICE IN THE DARJEELING HILLS

Initially, the tea plantations of Darjeeling hills had to face an acute shortage of labor. During those times, Darjeeling was sparsely populated. Plantation management had to procure labor from different parts of the country. Chotanagpur was the ultimate source of labor recruitment. The laborers were employed as bonded labor. But the laborers who were recruited from the Chotanagpur region faced difficulty to leave in the harsh winter seasons. As a result, the laborers often left the tea gardens during the winter season.

Later on, the management of tea plantation started recruiting laborers from Nepal and Sikkim, who could cope up with the erratic weather of the region.

In Darjeeling, the laborers were also recruited through *Sardars* and *Arkati*. In every garden, there were special teams of *Sardar* and *Arkati*. Once they brought labor into the garden, they would receive a cash incentive of Rs. 10 for each labor supplied. However, in Darjeeling, the system of recruitment was quite different from that of Dooars and Terai. In Darjeeling, the laborers were recruited and were required to serve like bonded laborers. Further to retain laborers in tea plantations, a para-military force named North Bengal Mounted Rifles (NBMR) was formed and their responsibilities were to keep surveillances on the movement of laborers (Sharma and Das, 2009). In Darjeeling, tea plantation management recruited *Sardars* from the local Gorkhas who were physically strong. They were entitled to receive their regular wages along with *Bakshis* for the recruitment of labor. The criterion for the recruitment of labor was physical fitness. However, the recruitment of labor in Darjeeling was characterized as coerced labor (Rinju, 2003).

Categories of Workers and Methods of Recruitments

In the tea plantation industry of North Bengal, mainly four categories of workers were involved: males, females, adolescents, and children (Sarker, 1992). Under the adolescent categories, male and female sub-categories exist. Earlier, the tea industry used to recruit child laborers, but recently recruitment of such labor has been completely stopped. Labor recruitment is done through different modes of recruitment. Permanent, casual, and contract are different modes of recruitment in tea plantations of this region. In case of the permanent mode of recruitment, only the dependent or the legal heir of the deceased person gets a job in that position. Hence, the number of job positions for permanent labor remains the same over the years. Casual workers are known as *Bigha* workers. *Bigha* workers are mainly recruited during the peak seasons. When the garden management recruits such as labor, the first persons to be given preference are the family members or dependents of the permanent workers. Other than these, few gardens sometimes also recruit contract laborers.

Criteria and Procedure for Recruitment of Labor

The permanent workers are recruited among the dependents or through replacements. As the number of job positions for permanent workers remains the same over the year, no new position is created. Table 4.3 depicts the job position of sample tea estates. However, the criteria for recruitment in such positions include the person should reach at least 16 years of age and should

Table 4.3 Sample Tea Estates and the Number of Permanent Laborers Position

Sl No.	Name of Sample Tea Estate	Number of Worker	Sl No.	Name of Sample Tea Estate	Number of Worker
1	Aibheel Tea Estate	2,146	18	Arya Tea Estate	381
2	Bagdogra Tea Estate	395	19	Ghatia Tea Estate	1,691
3	Baradighi Tea Estate	1,690	20	Kanchan View Tea Estate	112
4	Chaulluni Tea Estate	1,289	21	Matelli Tea Estate	1,764
5	Denguajhar Tea Estate	1,751	22	Mogulkata Tea Estate	1,116
6	Jadabpur Tea Estate	184	23	Moraghat Tea Estate	1,296
7	Jaldacca Altadanga Tea Estate	311	24	Nepuchapur Tea Estate	750
8	Jayantika Tea Estate	1,585	25	Phuguri Tea Estate	701
9	Kalabari Tea Estate	749	26	Radharani Tea Estate	424
10	Kathalguri Tea Estate	1,356	27	Ranicherra Tea Estate	1,372
11	Margaret's Hope Tea Estate	957	28	Saylee Tea Estate	1,616
12	Neora Nuddy Tea Estate	994	29	Telepara Tea Estate	1,312
13	Nuxalbari Tea Estate	676	30	Totapara Tea Estate	973
14	Raipur Tea Estate	617	31	New Dooars Tea Estate	1,778
15	Trisakti Tea Estate	159	32	Rangmukh and Cedar Tea Estate	1,717
16	Tumsong Tea Estate	449	33	Tindharia Tea Estate	316
17	Kamalpur Tea Estate	226			

Source: Field survey

be of sound health. The person should have to produce a medical certificate issued by the medical officer of that tea plantation to the plantation manager.

Bigha workers in the tea plantations are recruited from within the tea plantations and from outside the tea plantations. The process of recruitment for *Bigha* workers from within the tea estate involves a permanent worker (say, husband) whose dependent (wife) would be *a Bigha* worker; he (husband) has to apply to the plantation management. Then the plantation management would ask for a medical fitness certificate issued by the medical officer of that tea plantation. Then only it may recruit the *Bigha* worker. When the recruitment of *Bigha* workers is done from outside the plantations, the common practice is that the manager or his assistant would observe and ascertain the physical fitness of that person. In the case of contract labor, the common practice is only to allow the task to them by the garden authority and no specification is required. Thus, this is clear from the procedure of recruitment of labor: recruitment is based on the internal sources and there is no chance for an external candidate to be recruited in the tea plantation as permanent labor.

Promotions to the higher positions of tea garden laborers are rare in the tea plantations in the region. Only a few tea estates have promoted workers in higher positions. Those workers were promoted; their position changed to sub-staff and staff for rare cases only. No record exhibits regarding the promotion of workers to the managerial potion. So, it may be inferred that promotional opportunity is limited for the tea garden workers in Bengal (Mitra, 2010). However, those who were promoted to the staff and sub-staff positions were only male workers. The chance of promotion for male and female workers is not equal to an extent. For the male worker, the chance of promotion to a higher position is more than their counterpart (Bhadra, 2004). There are several factors behind it. The literacy rate, socio-economic condition, attitudes of planters, etc. are mainly considered. Due to the poor communication system between the labor colony and school, most of the parents are not interested to send their children to attend school. Although, as per the provision of the Plantation Labour Act, in every tea plantations, the arrangement of a school bus must be provided for school-going children, in practice the scenario is horrible. Primary schools in tea plantations are poorly maintained in this region. Most of the time, teachers are irregular and infrastructure is also not up to the standard. Under such deteriorated situations, parents of school-going children engage them in family care. Mostly, they are responsible to look after the young child of their families. Although, according to the Plantation Labour Act, there should be crèches in every tea plantations employing more than 30 women and should be maintained in a prescribed manner. But in reality, crèches are physically present but no other facilities are available. Thus, the girl child has limited opportunities to go to school. Hence, the social status of women in tea plantations is inferior due to their low level of literacy (Sarkar and Bhowmik, 1999).

References

Barua, P. (2008). *The tea industry of Assam: Origin and development.* Guwahati, India: EBH Publishers, p. 25.

Bhadra, M. (2004). Gender dimensions of tea plantation workers in West Bengal. *Indian Anthropologist,* 34(2), p. 44.

Ghosh, B. C. (1970). *Development of the tea industry in the district of Jalpaiguri 1869–1968.* Calcutta, India: Newman's Printers, p. 45.

Government of India. (1946). *Report on inquiry into conditions of labours in plantations in India.* New Delhi, India: Rage, D. Y., p. 76.

Government of India Report. (1966). *Report on the survey of labour conditions in tea plantations and factories in India 1961–1962.* Shimla, India: Ministry of Labour, p. 22.

Government of West Bengal. (2013). *Synopsis on Survey of Tea Gardens*. Kolkata, India: Joint Labour Commissioner, North Bengal Zone, p. 13.

Mitra, D. (2010). *Globalization and industrial relations in tea plantations*. New Delhi, India: Abhijeet Publication, p. 92.

Mitra, S. (2012). *Globalisation: Its impacts on industrial relations in tea plantation of Terai and Dooars region of West Bengal* (Doctoral thesis), University of North Bengal, Siliguri, India, p. 30. Retrieved from: http://shodhganga.inflibnet.ac.in/handle/10603/150726

Rinju, R. (2003). *Labour and health in tea plantations: A case study of Phuguri tea estate, Darjeeling* (Doctoral thesis), Jawaharlal Nehru University, New Delhi, India, p. 293. Retrieved from: http://shodhganga.inflibnet.ac.in/handle/10603/14985?mode=full

Sarkar, K., and Bhowmik, S. K. (1999). Trade unions and women workers in tea plantations. *Economic and Political Weekly*, 33(52), pp. 50–52.

Sarker, K. (1992). *Study of trade union organization among tea workers in Terai and Dooars region* (Doctoral thesis), University of North Bengal, Siliguri, India, pp. 37, 42. Retrieved from: http://shodhganga.inflibnet.ac.in/handle/10603/137111

Sharma, K., and Das, T. C. (2009). *Globalization and plantation workers in North East India*. Delhi, India: Kalpaz Publications, p. 67.

Urwick, L. F. (1938). *Scientific principles and organization*. New York, American Management Association, Institute of Management Series No. 19, 1938, p. 8.

Urwick, L. F. (1956). The manager's span of control. *Harvard Business Review*, June–July, p. 40.

5 Training and Compensation Practices of Tea Estates in North Bengal

Training for Tea Workers

The tea industry is a highly labor-intensive industry and huge labor is required across the year. Thus, due emphasis has been given on labor only. Hence, the training aspect of labor has been highlighted in this section.

To know the actual training scenario of tea workers in the North Bengal region, an attempt was made to investigate the sample tea estates of this region. However, a total of 33 sample tea estates were taken into consideration. The method of sample selection has been presented in the following.

With the aid of Raosoft software, we have determined the sample size, i.e., 33 tea estates. In the North Bengal region, there are 276 tea estates (Government of West Bengal, 2013). Hence, 276 tea estates were considered as population size for this purpose. Therefore, our sample size is 33, which is around 12 percent of the target population.

The stratified random sampling strategy has been adopted to select sample units. Stratifications have been made based on the ownership of the tea plantation. There are mainly four types of tea plantation companies that exist in this region. They are the Partnership Company, Public Limited Company, Proprietorship Company, and Public Sector Undertakings. Identification of sample tea estates has been shown in Table 5.1.

After the identification of sample tea estates, we have provided them a semi-structured feedback form. We have taken into consideration the feedback from managers of the concerned tea estates about the training facilities they are providing to their workers. However, summarization of their feedbacks has been presented in the subsequent sections.

In the tea estates of the North Bengal region, training is imparted to the workers only in certain specific areas. In this region, only 36 percent of the sample tea estates have training provisions for their workers. The training which is provided to workers by the tea plantation management in this region is not formal. In tea estates of this region, a wide range of training is offered to the workers. These include plucking, spraying, manure, weeding,

Table 5.1 Identifications of Sample Tea Estates

Ownership	Public Limited Company	Proprietorship Company	Partnership Company	Public Sector Undertakings	Total
Number of Tea Estates	142	116	10	8	276
Sample Size	16	13	2	2	33
Percent	11.26	11.20	20	25	11.95

Source: Author's own calculation.

pruning, planting, and the factory manufacturing process. Training is provided through 'off–the-job' and 'on-the-job' mode as well. In the case of 'on the job training' of tea workers, mentoring and coaching methods are preferred in most of the tea gardens. On the other hand, the lecture method is preferred in the case of off-the-job training. However, on-the-job-training methods are preferred in the tea estates. Tea workers are not usually literate and they like to learn while they are on work. On-the-job method of training has positive as well as negative impacts. The positive aspect of on-the-job' training is that it is less expensive and trainees learn while they are working, i.e., no working hours, i.e., man-days, is wasted. The negative aspect of this training method is that accidents sometimes happen while giving training on important or sensitive issues which proves costly for the tea estates.

OVERALL SCENARIO OF TRAINING PROGRAM

For the purpose of providing training to workers, the plantation management appoints the experienced senior employees of that plantation only. Usually, the practice is such that the manager or his assistant is responsible for providing training. Training sometimes takes the form of briefing. Before the start of the work, a manager or his assistant of the respective department takes a few minutes to convey his message to the workers. This practice is very common for plucking workers. Training is sometimes given by external experts. This kind of training takes place especially when new technology is adopted by the tea estates.

There is a higher need for a massive number of workers throughout the year in the tea plantations. Quality as well as quantity of tea fundamentally depends on the types of labor force deployed to the entire process. These labor forces should be trained enough on a variety of aspects of tea cultivation and production of the standard quality of tea. In addition to this, in recent time, a buzz word has arisen in the tea sector that is 'Ethical Tea

Partnership' (ETP). 'Ethical Tea Partnership' has immense influences on the world tea export market. Tea producers who are associated with 'Ethical Tea Partnership' are gaining added advantages. International buyers of tea demand for that quality of tea which has been produced under the guidelines of 'Ethical Tea Partnership'. 'Ethical Tea Partnership' primarily deals with sustainability in the tea industry in two ways. One is associated with the socio-economic status of workers and the other is the environmental aspect. Child labor, water conservation, conservation of soil, use of chemical and fertilizer, etc. are the essential codes for ETP. Since workers are the heart and soul of tea plantation, it is crucial to educate and train them regarding the various codes that have been prescribed by the ETP. But our study has suggested that 64 percent tea plantation in the North Bengal region has no scope of training. Since training is the weapon only in the hands of the plantation administration to educate and to make workers aware of the codes of ETP. Hence, our study signifies that the tea planters of Bengal have failed to abide by the ETP standards to a large extent. Further, it implies the uncertain market of tea produced from Bengal and also the uncertain future of the industry of this region.

However, in Table 5.2, an effort has been made to explain the positions of the tea companies based on the training program offered.

Table 5.2 shows that 33 sample tea plantations have been surveyed under the four types of Tea Company. It exhibits that the Proprietorship Tea Company occupies the topmost position in terms of the training program. Under the Proprietorship category, 13 plantations have been surveyed, out of which 7 plantations have a training program for their workers, which constitute about 53.84 percent. The Partnership Tea Company occupies the second position in this respect. Under The Partnership Tea Company, two

Table 5.2 Percentage of Training Program Among Tea Plantations

SL No:	Types of Tea Company	Number of Tea Plantation Surveyed	Providing Training	Percentage (%)	Rank
1.	Public Limited Tea Company	16	4	25%	3
2.	Proprietorship Tea Company	13	7	53.84%	1
3.	Public Sector Undertakings Tea Company	2	0	0%	4
4.	Partnership Tea Company	2	1	50%	2

Source: Field survey.

plantations have been surveyed, out of which one plantation has a training facility, which implies that 50 percent tea plantations have training provisions. Subsequently, under the Public Limited Tea Company, about 25 percent of tea plantations have training provisions. On the contrary, the Public Sector Undertakings Tea Company has no training provision for its workers.

Modes of Training

Modes of training imply the way or process by which trainees acquire knowledge, attitudes, and set of skills in their current jobs. In our study, we asked the plantation management how they provide training to their workers. However, based on the feedback of respondents, the detailed accounts of modes of training in tea plantations have been presented in Table 5.3.

Table 5.3 depicts the modes of the training program adopted by the different tea plantation companies in the North Bengal region. We have observed that only 12 tea plantations out of 33 sample tea plantations have a training program for their workers. These 12 tea plantations fall under different types of tea plantation companies. However, we know that there are lots of modes of training under 'on-the-job' and 'off-the-job' training methods. The table shows that five tea plantations have the combination of Coaching and Mentoring modes of training, which constitute about 41.66 percent. Three tea plantations have Mentoring modes of training, which constitute 25 percent, and two tea plantations have Mentoring and Job Rotation modes of training, which constitute 16.66 percent. One tea plantation provides a Coaching model of training, which is 8.33 percent, and finally, Lectures and Conferences modes are provided by one tea plantation, which is also 8.33 percent.

However, this undoubtedly signifies from the earlier discussion that Coaching and Mentoring modes of training are the most preferred in the tea plantation of this locale. Coaching and Mentoring come under the on-the-job

Table 5.3 Modes of Training Provided by the Sample Tea Plantations

SL No.	Modes of Training	Number of Plantations	Percentage	Cumulative Percentage
1.	Mentoring	3	25	25
2.	Coaching	1	8.33	33.33
3.	Coaching & Mentoring	5	41.67	75
4.	Mentoring & Job Rotation	2	16.67	91.67
5.	Lectures & Conferences	1	8.33	100

Source: Field survey.

training method. This method of training is most preferred because workers in tea plantations like to work under someone's supervision who guides them at the time of work.

Measurement of Effectiveness of Training Program

To measure the effectiveness of the training program initiated by different types of tea companies, the overall performance of workers before participating and after participating in training program has been taken into consideration. For this purpose, an individual garden has been considered as a sample unit. Managers of sample tea plantations have been interviewed. They were asked about the performance of trainees before attending the training program and after attending the training program. However, we have identified seven areas where training is imparted. These are Plucking, Manure, Weeding, Spraying, Pruning, Planting, and Manufacturing. A five-point Likert Scale has been used for this purpose. Based on the nature of the collected data, the Wilcoxon sign ranks test has been used.

Wilcoxon signed ranks test is one of the non-parametric tests. This is like a paired sample *t*-test, but it is used while the assumption of paired sample *t*-test is violated. One of the most central assumptions of paired sample *t*-test is that the data should be normally distributed. In the study, first, we have examined the normality of the collected data, and based on the result of the normality test, we have preceded the subsequent statistical test for each type of tea plantation company.

I.   PROPRIETORSHIP TEA COMPANY

We have conducted the Shapiro-Wilk test to check the normality on the sample data set. However, we have observed that the calculated *p*-value of the Shapiro-Wilk test in case of after training and before training are 0.022 and 0.034, respectively, which are below 5 percent level of significance. Hence, the null hypothesis, i.e., the data is normal, has been rejected. Now, based on the result of the normality test, the decision has been taken that paired sample *t*-test cannot be performed by this data set. Hence, the substitute test of paired sample *t*-test, i.e., Wilcoxon signed ranks test, is appropriate.

WILCOXON SIGNED RANKS TEST

Null Hypothesis (Ho): There is no significant disparity between the performance of workers before providing training and after providing training.

We have found that that the mean values of the same set of data are different in respect of time. The mean values of 'After training' and 'Before

Table 5.4 Test Statistics

	Before training—After training
Z	−2.530
Asymp. Sig. (2-tailed)	0.011

training' are 24.5714 and 20.7143, respectively. The standard deviation is also found to be different: 'Before training' it was 2.05866 and 'After training' it was 2.14920. This is lucid that the training program has an impact on the performance of the workers; i.e., the average performance has improved after attaining the training program. But to confirm if the mean's difference is statistically important or not, Test Statistics is shown in Table 5.4. In the table, the significant p-value is shown.

The table exposes that the computed Z value of the Wilcoxon Signed Ranks test is 0.011, which is less than 5 percent level of significance. Therefore, we have rejected the null hypothesis.

Thus, we can assert that there is a significant dissimilarity between the performance of workers before providing training and after providing training. Finally, we may assert that the training program for tea workers has great influences on enhancing workers present job performances.

II. PUBLIC LIMITED TEA COMPANY

We have conducted the Shapiro-Wilk test to check the normality on the sample data set.

The calculated p-value of the Shapiro-Wilk test in case of after training and before training are 0.048 and 0.045, respectively, which are below 0.05. Hence, the null hypothesis, i.e., the data is normal, has been rejected. The outcome of normality inferred that paired sample t-test cannot be performed by this data set. Hence, Wilcoxon signed ranks test is appropriate.

WILCOXON SIGNED RANKS TEST

Null Hypothesis (Ho): There is no significant distinction between the performance of workers before and after providing training.

We have observed the descriptive statistics which shows that the mean values of the two related data set are different in respect of time. The mean values of 'After training' and 'Before training' are 21 and 18.50, respectively. This is apparent that the training program has an impact on the performance of the workers; i.e., the average performance of workers has

Table 5.5 Test Statistics

	Before training—After training
Z	−1.857
Asymp. Sig. (2-tailed)	0.063

improved after the training program. But to confirm if the mean's difference is statistically important or not, Test Statistics is shown in Table 5.5. In the table, the significant *p*-value is shown.

The table exposes that the computed Z value of the Wilcoxon Signed Ranks test is 0.063, which is more than 5 percent level of significance. Therefore, we have accepted the null hypothesis.

Thus, we can assert that there is no significant dissimilarity between the performance of workers before providing training and after providing training. This further confirms that the training program provided by the Public Limited tea companies are not effective.

III.   PARTNERSHIP TEA COMPANY

Under the Partnership Tea Company, only one sample tea plantation has been surveyed. Therefore, we do not have any scope of statistical analysis. Hence we have taken into consideration the data of individual tea plantation for this purpose: i.e., an individual tea garden is a sample unit. The manager's opinion about the average performance of all workers before training and after training has been considered. However, according to the manager, workers' average performance score before training was 23, and after training, it stood at 27.

From this score, it can be generalized that the training program is effective enough. Further, Partnership Tea Companies in the North Bengal region has been benefited through the workers' training program.

Performance Appraisal

In some of the tea gardens in the North Bengal region, the practice of performance appraisal is found to be in existence. But the existing system is not organized in nature. Each tea estate has got its method of appraising the performance of its workers. The common practice of performance evaluation in the tea estates is confined to the plucking of leaves and factory works. Some of the tea estates appraise the performance of their workers on a monthly, quarterly, or half-yearly basis. In most of the cases, it has been found that the management of tea plantation uses the performance appraisal system for reward allocation. Some also use the performance appraisal system for the identification of training needs.

Compensation

Wage for Tea Workers

The rate of the wage of the tea garden workers is revised from time to time. Since the inception of the tea industry in Bengal, the rate of wage paid to workers had not been followed by any rational parameter. Earlier, there was a difference in the amount of wage paid to the female and male workers. Such a difference was observed greater during the pre-independence time. Before 1966, the differences in the amount of wage between male and female workers were 14 paisa. This difference was raised to 17 paisa after the recommendation of Wage Boards and was continued till the enactment of the Equal Remuneration Act, 1976 (Rai, 2015). However, subsequently, such difference was declined but the attitude of the planters remained the same in the case of determination of wage rate. Plantation management's argument in favor of such a detrimental difference was that women were not regarded equal with their counterparts in the workplace and maintaining equality would lead to discrimination against men (Bhowmik, 1981).

The first increment of wages in tea plantations in West Bengal was started in 1962. In the Darjeeling and Terai regions, the wage rates for males, females, and children were Rs. 1.95, Rs. 1.81, and Rs. 1.07, respectively. On the contrary, in the Dooars region, the wage rates for males, females, and children were Rs. 1.98, Rs. 1.84, and Rs. 1.07, respectively (Rai, 2015). From the beginning of the increment system of the wage for the tea labor in the study region, discrimination prevailed. The discrimination of wage payment was based on both region and gender basis. However, this increment was only 6 paisa for women and 8 paisa for men based on the previous rate of wage. Another discrimination of wage rate was based on the size of the tea plantation. The usual practice was that the plantations in size less than 500 acres, workers will receive 3 paisa lower than the normal rate of wage.

In 1966, the Central Wage Board made recommendations that the normal rate of wage should be raised by 13 paisa for men, 10 paisa for women, and 7 paisa for children (Bhadra, 1997). This recommendation of the apex institution further proves that the discrimination of wage was in existence in the tea plantations of North Bengal region. In Table 5.6, a brief account of revision of wage in this region has been presented.

It can be observed from the table that the amount of wages for tea garden workers has been increased gradually. The demand of trade unions and bipartite meetings was the prime mechanism for incrementing the wage of tea

Table 5.6 Revision of Wage for the Tea Worker of North Bengal

Year	Men	Women	Child
1969–1970	2.39	2.22	1.29
1970–1971	2.48	2.31	1.33
1971–1972	2.71	2.54	1.45
1972–1973	2.94	2.77	1.56
1973–1978	5.24	5.07	2.73

Source: Combination statistics of Biswas (2011) and Rai (2015)

workers until 1975. In 1978, the wage was raised as per the recommendation of the Minimum Wage Fixation Committee. Many employers during that time did not accept this recommendation made by the committee (Bhadra, 1997).

Presently, the existing wage rate of tea workers in the tea plantations of North Bengal is Rs. 132.50 per day. On the other hand, the approved minimum wage for the unskilled worker of agricultural activities is Rs. 220 (without food) in West Bengal (with effect from 1st July 2017). As per the nature of work, tea workers possess at least a few quantities of skills and thus they should be in the semi-skilled group (Biswas, 2016). In the case of semi-skilled activities in agriculture, the prescribed existing minimum wage rate is Rs. 252 per day (without food) in West Bengal. Hence, tea plantation workers of West Bengal received about half of the approved minimum wage. However, the management of tea plantations argued in this regard that they pay fringe benefits in addition to the basic wage which amounts to Rs. 142.94 for Terai and Dooars and Rs. 144.60 for Darjeeling. As per their calculation, the cost per worker has been presented in Table 5.7:

Table 5.7 Wage and Fringe Benefits for Permanent Tea Workers of North Bengal Region

Particulars	Dooars region	Terai region	Darjeeling region
BASIC WAGE RATE (as on 1.1.17)	132.50	132.50	132.50
FRINGE BENEFITS A. Non-statutory			
1. Foodgrains	14.20	14.20	14.20
2. Dry Tea	3.54	3.54	5.20
3. Fuel, etc.	5.55	5.55	5.55
4. Addl. Comp/Pay of Post	8.50	8.50	8.50

Particulars	Dooars region	Terai region	Darjeeling region
Total non-statutory	**31.79**	**31.79**	**33.45**
B. PLA Statutory			
5. Housing Facilities	14.71	14.71	14.71
6. Education Facilities	2.73	2.73	2.73
7. Medical Facilities (sick and maternity)	16.19	16.19	16.19
8. Earned Leave	14.46	14.46	14.46
9. Welfare Facilities	5.41	5.41	5.41
Total Statutory	**53.50**	**53.50**	**53.50**
C. Common Statutory			
10. Provident Fund	19.51	19.51	19.51
11. Bonus- 20%	31.09	31.09	31.09
12. Gratuity	7.05	7.05	7.05
Total Common Statutory	**57.65**	**57.65**	**57.65**
D. Total Fringe Benefits	**142.94**	**142.94**	**144.60**
TOTAL WAGE COST	**275.44**	**275.44**	**277.10**

Source: Field survey and combination of various statistics of Indian Tea Association, Kolkata, 2017.

The table indicates the cost of the wage for a tea worker in the North Bengal region. The total wage cost for a worker is Rs. 275.44 both in Dooars and Terai region and Rs. 277.10 in the Darjeeling region. In the Darjeeling region, the wage cost for a worker is a little higher than of the Dooars and Terai. This wage difference is mainly because of the cost of dry tea provided to the workers at a subsidized price. Since the market price of the Darjeeling tea is more than the price of tea from the Dooars and the Terai. The total wage cost and its various components have been shown in the table are completely based on the calculations of the employer of tea estates. However, the actual practice is exclusively different. The amount of basic wage provided to the worker is fixed for the entire North Bengal region but the other components of wage are varying from plantation to plantation.

According to the workers union, the amount for non-statutory benefits included with the wage cost is partially payable by the employers. Their logic is that since the State Government is providing food grains at the subsidized rate to the entire family employed in the plantation area; there are ample sources of fuel from nature in and around plantation areas and for this purpose, not a single paisa is paid by employers. Dry tea is only provided by employers and other items are provided irregularly. So, the cost of such items should be deducted from the total cost of wages. In the case of common statutory benefits, most of the time the rate of bonus provided is lower than 20 percent. Provident Fund and Gratuity remain due for long almost for every tea plantation. Hence, the calculation of total wage cost is not justified and it should be much lower than that of Rs. 275.44 for Dooars and Terai and Rs. 277.10 for Darjeeling.

In reality, the rate of wage for tea workers in Bengal is inferior in India. The daily rate of wage for tea plantation workers in Kerala is Rs. 310, in Karnataka is Rs. 263 and in Tamil Nadu is Rs. 241. In the case of West Bengal, even if all costs of the fringe benefits are added, the amount of wage would be extreme below the Southern States of India. The average auction price of tea from Kerala, Karnataka, and Tamil Nadu was Rs. 115.48, Rs. 99.07, and Rs. 93.07, respectively. Surprisingly, on the other hand, the average auction price of tea from West Bengal was Rs. 128.54 (Tea Board of India, 2017).

This is clear to us that the tea industry of Bengal is in a better position in terms of auction price and at the same time planters are paying a lower wage to workers. Despite the poor auction price of tea, South Indian tea planters are paying the prescribed rate of minimum wages to workers. The tea planters of West Bengal, on the other hand, pay and fix wage rates through the mechanisms of collective bargaining or tripartite agreement though they have a better profitable position than the South Indian tea industry. Hence, the usual claim made by the planters of Bengal of lower profitability which makes them difficult to pay minimum rates of wages cannot be said to be justified.

However, the determination of the wage rate in the tea industry of Bengal is made through the tripartite agreement in which representatives of trade unions, representatives of planters associations, and representatives from the government are present. Usually, once in three years, the representatives are decided mutually to secure the minimum rate of wage. Some of the memoranda regarding the settlement of the wage rate are presented in Table 5.8.

As per the Memorandum of Settlement dated 21 July 1994 in respect of daily wages of plantation workers, the rate of increase of daily wages per day is as follows:

Table 5.8 Memorandum of Settlement of Wage Rate on 21.07.1994

S. L. No	Period	Nominal Wage Per Day
1.	With effect from 01.04.1994	Rs. 2.50
2.	With effect from 01.04.1995	Rs. 2.50
3.	With effect from 01.04.1996	Rs. 2.00

Source: Combination of various statistics of Indian Tea Association and Labour Department, Government of West Bengal.

Table 5.9 Memorandum of Settlement of Wage Rate on 25.07.2005

S. L. No	Period	Nominal Wage Per Day
1.	With effect from 01.04.05	Rs. 2.50
2.	With effect from 01.04.06	Rs. 2.50
3.	With effect from 01.04.07	Rs. 3.00

Source: Combination of various statistics of Indian Tea Association and Labour Department, Government of West Bengal.

As per the Memorandum of Settlement dated 25 July 2005 in respect of daily wages of plantation workers, the rate of increase of daily wages per day is as follows (Table 5.9).

As per the tripartite Memorandum of Settlement dated 20 February 2015 between the tea managements and representatives of trade unions, the nominal wage at the end of each period along with incremental wage hike is as given in Table 5.10.:

Table 5.10 Memorandum of Settlement of Wage Rate on 20.02.2015

S. L. No	Period	Nominal wage per day
1	From 01/04/2014 to 31/03/2015	Rs. 112.50 (increment of Rs 17.50)
2	From 01/04/2015 to 31/03/2016	Rs. 122.50 (increment of Rs 10)
3	From 01/04/2016 to 31/03/2017	Rs. 132.50 (increment of Rs 10)

Source: Combination of various statistics of Indian Tea Association and Labour Department, Government of West Bengal.

In the Table 5.11, a brief outline of yearly wage along with its percentage changes has been presented:

Table 5.11 Yearly Wages and Its Percentage of Growth

Year	Wage in Rs.	Percentage of Growth
2001	45.9	–
2002	49.9	8.714597
2003	54	8.216433
2004	54	0
2005	56.5	4.62963
2006	59	4.424779

(*Continued*)

Table 5.11 (Continued)

Year	Wage in Rs.	Percentage of Growth
2007	62	5.084746
2008	66.1	6.612903
2009	70.6	6.807867
2010	75.1	6.373938
2011	75.1	0
2012	85	13.18242
2013	90	5.882353
2014	95	5.555556
2015	112.5	18.42105
2016	122.5	8.888889
2017	132.5	8.163265

Source: Combination data of Labour Department of West Bengal, 2017.

Table 5.11 clearly illustrates the growth of wages for tea workers in Bengal over the years. The growth pattern is observed zigzag. From 2001 to 2011, it is found that the percentage changes in the number of wage moves below 10 percent. Surprisingly, a notable change, i.e., 13.18 percent, is found in 2012. There is a genuine clue behind this sudden change in the wage rate. This is because of changes in Government in West Bengal. The year 2011 was the period of political transition in Bengal. During that period, the political condition was in serious turmoil. Due to this condition, no change was made in 2011. However, at the end of this year on 4 November 2011, a memorandum of settlement of wage was signed. Hence, the actual implication of this settlement of wages did not take place in 2011, although, it was mentioned in the settlement that the implication of this would begin from 1 April 2011. However, the ruling government then realized the need to improve the conditions of labor and made a notable change in daily wages in 2012. Again, the ruling government, before the election in the state assembly of 2016 in Bengal, brought a drastic change in the wage rate (18.42 percent) in 2015. In the history of tea industry of Bengal, this wage growth of 18.42 percent is undoubtedly a record.

So, it may be concluded that the changes in the wage rate in the tea industry of Bengal are directly linked with the political influences to a large extent. However, in Figure 5.1, a trend line has been presented for the easy representation of wage growth.

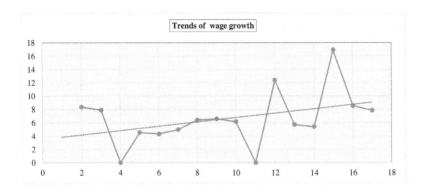

Figure 5.1 Trends of Wage Growth

The figure reveals that the growth of the wage rate of tea workers of Bengal over the phase of time has followed typical randomness. From this trend of wage growth, we cannot infer any conclusions until it is statistically proved. Hence, it is imperative to justify statistically, whether the sequence of observations of the growth rate of wage over the period is random or not. However, in the following Run test (Shown in Table 5.12), it confirms the randomness of wage growth.

Run Test

H_0: The growth rate of wages is random.

Table 5.12 Run Test

Year	Wage	Percentage Change	Sign of Change
2001	45.9	–	
2002	49.9	8.714597	
2003	54	8.216433	
2004	54	0	– Run 1
2005	56.5	4.62963	+ Run 2
2006	59	4.424779	– Run 3
2007	62	5.084746	+
2008	66.1	6.612903	+
2009	70.6	6.807867	+Run 4

(*Continued*)

Table 5.12 (Continued)

Year	Wage	Percentage Change	Sign of Change
2010	75.1	6.373938	–
2011	75.1	0	– Run 5
2012	85	13.18242	+ Run 6
2013	90	5.882353	–
2014	95	5.555556	– Run 7
2015	112.5	18.42105	+ Run 8
2016	122.5	8.888889	–
2017	132.5	8.163265	– Run 9
$\|Z\|$ –Statistics = $\dfrac{\|r - \mu\|}{\sigma}$		Positive Run (n_1) = 6 Negative Run (n_2) = 8 Total Run (r) = 9 **Calculated $\|Z\|$ = 0.65**	

The calculated z value is = **0.65**

At a 5 percent level of significance, the tabulated value of $|Z|$ statistics is 1.96. Since the calculated value of $|Z|$ is less than the tabulated value, the null hypothesis has been accepted. Hence, a conclusion can be drawn based on the Run test that the sequence of the growth rate of wage is random.

Since 2001, the wage growth rate for workers of the tea industry in the Bengal region has not followed a systematic pattern. It is preferred that the wage growth rate should follow a systematic pattern. Since we know that the growth of wage or salary in the organized sector is based on the consumer price index. In the case of the tea industry of Bengal, wage growth is based on political influences. Even the wage for tea workers is based on the prescribed minimum wages of the state, due to which the wage growth pattern observed is volatile. These are the probable reasons behind the sudden strikes, closures, and lockouts of tea estates in Bengal, thus making the industry vulnerable.

Mode of Payment of Wage

In the ancient period, wage was paid to the tea workers of Darjeeling and Dooars through two modes: through the *Sardar* and directly to the laborers. Workers employed by the *Sardar* were paid through the *Sardar*. Commissions were paid by the planters to the *Sardar* for their intermediate jobs. For the *Nij Putty Collies*, i.e., workers who joined work on their own, wages were given directly by plantation management. However, the *Sardary* system of labor recruitment and wage payment no longer existed in the tea industry of Bengal. In present times, the wage is being paid directly to the workers by the plantation management. Amount of wage is paid to the workers of tea plantation either fortnightly or on a weekly basis. In most of the tea plantations of this region, the amount of wage is paid within three days of ending the last wage period.

In Dooars, only one garden is found to be paying workers' wages directly into their bank account. The garden has reported that only 60 percent of their workers' payment is made through bank account transfer. The rest of the tea gardens pay wages to the workers through a direct cash payment mode. In the case of direct cash payment, workers acknowledge the receipt by putting their thumb impression or signature. After the demonetization, initiatives were made for every tea estate to pay wage through direct account transfer. However, due to the poor banking infrastructure in the North Bengal region, the initiatives were in vain.

Bonus of Tea Workers in Bengal

Earlier, tea plantation workers received a bonus as per the North East India Tea Plantation Bonus Agreement (NEITPBA), 1961. This system continued till 1963. Before that in Dooars, tea workers demanded about 60 days' average wage of the year 1953 as the amount of bonus of 1954. In the same year, the West Bengal Cha Sramik Union (WBCSU) threatened to go on strike on the same issue. It is crucial to note that in 1954, the industry earned a huge profit. However, initially, the employers opposed the demand raised by the workers. Then they applied to government regarding their inability to pay bonuses as per the demand of the workers. However, finally, the bonus was paid by them unwillingly as they had no other option at that time. Thus, since then industry-wise bonus agreement was reached through the intervention of the central government and many organizations faced serious problems by this liability.

After 1956, the Government of India appointed a sub-committee of bonuses. A new system of calculation of bonus was introduced by the planters of Assam in 1959. Finally, in 1965 the Payment of Bonus Act was passed. At present in the tea plantation industry, the bonus is paid at the rate of 8.33 percent of workers' yearly earnings, and in addition to that an ex gratia up to 11.67 percent of yearly earnings, which total up to 20 percent.

However, in the financial year 2011–2012, the majority of the tea estates in the Nort Bengal region (236) paid a bonus to their workmen at 20 percent.

The rates of bonus paid by the other tea estates to their workmen in this region are as follows:

1 Tea estate paid at 19.5%
1 Tea estate paid at 19 %
7 Tea estates paid at 18%
3 Tea estates paid at 17%
4 Tea estates paid at 16%
2 Tea estates paid at 15.5%
3 Tea estates paid at 15%
1 Tea estate paid at 14.5%
1 Tea estate paid at 14%
2 Tea estates paid at 12%
2 Tea estates paid at 11%
7 Tea estates paid at 10%
2 Tea estates paid at 9%
2 Tea estates paid at 8.33%

Incentives

In the tea plantation industry of Bengal, the system of incentive wage is found to be prevalent, in the tea plantations and the factories of the tea estate. The nature of incentives in the case of plantation and the manufacturing factory is found to be distinct from one another. For the factory, the incentive is calculated on the basis of added working hours spent by workers. In plantations, on the other hand, an incentive is calculated based on the added task. The task for the plantation workers implies the plucking quantity of tea leaves. However, the determination of tasks varies from tea estate to tea estate. The measurement of tasks of the hill and plain regions is widely varied. Tasks also varied from season to season. Similarly, the rate per extra task is also different. The usual practice is, for example, a worker is required to pluck 30 kilograms of leaves. If someone plucks beyond that limit, he or she is entitled to get Rs. 4 per extra per kilogram. The calculation of incentives for the factory worker in the tea estate of this region is based on the extra hours they work. Workers in this region working beyond the stipulated hours are entitled to receive a double rate of the normal working hour in case of Public Sector Undertakings. Otherwise, Rs. 35 per extra hour is paid by tea estates under DBITA (Doors Branch of Indian Tea Association).

References

Bhadra, M. (1997). Women workers in tea plantations. In Bhadra, R. K. & Bhadra, M. (Eds.), *Plantation labours of North-East India* (pp. 191–192). Dibrugarh, India: N.L. Publishers.

Bhowmik, S. (1981). *Class formation in the plantation system.* New Delhi, India: People's Publishing House, p. 94.

Biswas, D. (2016). Wage determination machinery of tea industry in India: A case of west Bengal state. *Journal of Tea Science Research*, 6(8), p. 1. https://doi.org/10.5376/jtsr.2016.06.0008

Government of West Bengal. (2013). *Synopsis on survey of tea gardens.* Kolkata, India: State Labour Institute, p. 5.

Rai, S. (2015). *Plantation industry of Darjeeling region: A historical study* (Doctoral thesis), Sikkim University, Sikkim, India, pp. 70–71. Retrieved from: http://14.139.206.50:8080/jspui/bitstream/1/3113/1/Susma%20Rai.pdf

Tea Board of India. (2017). *State wise tea price in E-Auctions during 2017.* Retrieved from: http://www.teaboard.gov.in/pdf/Statewise_Auction_Prices_2017_website_pdf3178.pdf

6 Integration and Maintenance Function in Tea Estates of North Bengal

Integration Function

The integration function of human resource management consists of workers' participation in management, collective bargaining, conflict resolution, establishing good relations in the organization, promoting good quality of work-life, etc.

In the tea industry of West Bengal, the participation of workers in decision making is not in practice. In the decision-making process of tea estates, only the top-level management of the organization participates actively. Management of the tea estate feels reluctant to establish good relations with laborers. Some kind of negligence toward laborers is still present in the mind of management of the tea estate. There is a huge social difference between the two parties. This social difference is prevalent since the inception of the industry. At the outset of the industry, the British tea planters regarded workers as *Coolie*. A similar attitude still prevails in tea estates of this region. The quality of the work-life of tea workers has also remained the same over the decades.

Industrial Relations

For the advancement and growth of any business, it is necessary to build a strong and melodious industrial relations. There are core three actors which are unswervingly concerned in industrial relations, viz. employees, government, and employers. In India, industrial relations are administered by multifarious labor legislations.

In North Bengal, trade union movement began only after around 90 years of the establishment of the first tea garden in 1856. On 15 September 1945, the first union, Darjeeling Tea Garden Worker's Union, was established under the leadership of Ratanlal Brahmin, Sushil Chatterjee, and B.B. Chettri (Prasanneswari, 1984). Ironically, the trade union movement began around the period of independence of our nation. The reason behind the late inception of the trade union movement in West Bengal was the non-existence of the proper condition for the growth of trade unions. The tea workers were not united and hence lacked the bargaining power. They were illiterate and too poor. They had no contact with the outside world. On the other hand, tea planters were well organized. They took full advantage of the poor workers who could not raise their voice against the planters. Thus, the relationship existed like master and servant. As a result, they were paid poorly and had to work in unhealthy working conditions. Meanwhile, the planters were well aware about huge labor agitations which were sweeping throughout the country under the leadership of nationalist. Planters made their possible efforts to prevent the penetration of such agitation into tea gardens. Restrictions were made by the planters. Trade union leaders from outside were not allowed in the garden and workers were not permitted to meet any outside trade union leaders. For this purpose, the planter of this region formed a private armed force, which was known as North Bengal Mounted Rifles. However, by 1946, the entire scenario began to change. The trade union movement slowly began to penetrate the tea gardens of Bengal. Thus, new hopes and aspirations rose among the workers. It is believed that trade union in the tea gardens of Bengal was induced first by the Communist party in 1946 and the entire credit for this success goes to Mr. Ratanlal Brahman. The history of the trade union in the tea industry of Bengal marked its first strike on 18 June 1946. On this day, the Chai Camman Majdur Union placed 'strike notice' to the management of 13 tea gardens for their seven-point demands. Their demands included recognition of trade unions, increase wage rate, better medical facilities, ration at a lower rate, dearness allowance at 25 percent of total wage, and the abolition of *the Hattabahar* system (Mitra, 2010).

We can imagine the condition of tea workers in absence of trade unions during this long period. It is relevant to note in this connection that peaceful industrial relations existed during this period. Due to the nonappearance of trade unions, which is one of the prime actors of industrial relations, workers were dominated by the planters. The planters dictated both the wages and the condition of works and were indulged in extensive exploitation of the workers, who were weak, uneducated, and unorganized. However, the state of affairs was distorted drastically after the commencement of trade unions in the tea sector of Bengal. Workers were organized and conscious of their rights. Subsequently, the industry began witness the gigantic labor campaigning in the form of gheraos, lockout, strike, etc.

In India, industrial relations are governed by labor legislation. Among diverse labor legislations enacted so far, the Plantation Labour Act, 1951, was one of the strategic turning points to the labor unions in the tea industry. This Act made compulsory to provide multifarious welfare measures, which include housing, health care, education, drinking water, crèches, etc., to workers. The Factories Act, 1948, also played an important role in labor legislations. This Act governs the working conditions of workers in factories. Further, it provides detailed guidelines regarding the health, safety, and welfare of workers along with annual leave with wages and working hours of different types of workforces like adults, children, women, and adolescents. However, the Plantation Labour Act, 1951, the Factories Act, 1948, the Payment of Gratuity Act, 1972, the Payment of Bonus Act, 1965, etc. were enacted after the independence to regulate the relations between workers and their employers. Meanwhile, the Great Depression due to the World War II sent back foot to the planters. During this period, the relationship between labor and management deteriorated to a large extent. Apart from these, the industrial relation system in the early days of independence sought to control conflicts and disputes through the enactment of such extreme labor legislation. All labor laws were protective for the workers and the prime objectives were to safeguard the workers' interest. This protectionist policy was responsible for creating an atmosphere that led to an increase in inefficiency in firms over employment. Due to this, the trade unions became more aggressive. Thus, they made unreasonable demands and resorted to strike frequently. This brought about bitter industrial relations in the tea plantation industry of this region. However, as of now, the relationship between management and labor in the tea industry of Bengal is unstable. Professor D. Mitra, a profound scholar in the field of labor management relations, stated that globalization is mainly liable for the unhealthy relations present in the tea industry of Bengal. Evidence shows that the average number of strikes, gheraos, gate meeting, lockout, etc. have amplified drastically only after globalization. Workers of tea estates have lost their faith in plantation management. Workers, backed by unions, raised their demands repeatedly in such a way that managers and other staff left the tea estates. Thus, the tea industry of North Bengal is now in deep turmoil.

Operating Trade Unions in Tea Estates of North Bengal

As per the report published by the State Labour Institute (SLI), Govt. of West Bengal (2013), there are 22 operating trade unions in the tea industry of North Bengal. The tea estate-wise representation of trade unions is presented in the following manner:

• 90 tea estates have a single union
• 42 tea estates have two unions

- 45 tea estates have three unions
- 28 tea estates have four unions
- 36 tea estates have five unions
- 20 tea estates have six unions
- 11 tea estates have seven unions
- 1 tea estate has nine unions

Collective Bargaining

Collective bargaining is a typical process of discussions between the management and workers, intended at reaching concurrence that is aimed at adjusting the working environment.

Collective bargaining exists vigorously in the tea plantation of Bengal. Collective bargaining serves as the most influential mechanism for fixing wage and bonus rates for tea workers. Tea workers of this part of the Indian tea industry raise their voices collectively on account of several issues like a bonus, ration, electricity, housing, etc. (Duara, 2015). Collective voice raised by tea workers in Bengal on wage issues is a regular and common phenomenon. Hence, collective bargaining is one of the key features of tea plantation management. Tea plantations of Bengal have a mainly bipartite and tripartite mechanism for settlement of collective issues.

There are definite prototypes that are followed in the practice of collective bargaining machinery. The common practice is that trade unions present their demands to the employer in a written form containing the issues thereon. The demands may be a hike in wage rate, rate of incentives, percentage of the bonus, overtime rate, etc. The employers' organization then initiates the bipartite-level discussion. However, if the issues demanded by the trade union are not resolved at this bipartite-level discussion, then the same is sent to the appropriate authority, i.e., state government. The state government then communicates with the parties involved and instigates tripartite talks. In the process of tripartite discussions, representatives of government, owner, and union are present. Thus, the discussion is carried on until they arrive at an amicable settlement to an aggrieved point (Sarkar, 2015).

Maintenance Function

The maintenance function is designed to look after and encourage the intellectual as well as the bodily health of workers. For this purpose, the organization arranges good quality working conditions, safety and security at work, leisure facilities, recreation and leave, housing, health check-up, etc.

Welfare of the Tea Plantation Workers

The concept of 'labor welfare' is dynamic. Multifarious dimensions of labor welfare enable laborers to maintain a portly and comfortable life. Consequently, it leads to higher productivity of labor and proficiency of an enterprise. It also amplifies the value of the existing laborers by circuitously releasing the compulsion on their purse. The Plantation Labour Act ensures the welfare of the laborers by way of providing facilities such as canteens, crèches, transportation, recreation, education for the children, suitable housing accommodation of plantation workers and for their families in and around the workplaces of the plantation, etc.

The word 'welfare' means the status of well-being, happiness, good health, comfort, protection, safety, etc.

In general, the term implies that the deliberate efforts made for the advancement of the individuals or community (Ghosh, 2006). The betterment of individuals or groups of individuals somehow relates to physical, mental, emotional, etc. The efforts may be shaped by the government, NGOs, business organizations, and the like (Das, 2009). On the other hand, the recipients of such efforts may be the individuals or groups of individuals or class. Specifically, labor welfare means the efforts made by the employer, government, trade unions, and other agencies for the upswing of the social conditions of laborers (Flippo, 1984).

In the case of tea plantations of North Bengal, tea planters provide various facilities to satisfy the Plantation Labour Act (PLA), 1951 (Bhowmik, 1981). The Plantation Labour Act (PLA), 1951, provides guidelines for the plantation laborers to the planters regarding welfare facilities. The Act guides that the employer has to provide housing facilities for all permanent workers and their families, educational facilities for their children, medical facilitates for workers and families, effective arrangements of drinking water for the workers, canteen facility, crèches facility, and recreational facility.

Besides these statutory welfare measures for the plantation laborers, there are certain other non-statutory welfare benefits given by the employers. These non-statutory benefits are mainly based on the demand that workers submit through the union to the employer. Such non-statutory benefits are concessional/subsidized food grains, fuel (firewood), umbrella, slippers, tarpaulin, kambal (blanket), etc. (Mitra, 2010).

Housing Facilities

Section 15 of the Act prescribes that every employer has to provide suitable housing accommodation for all permanent workers who are employed in the plantation. It has been noticed that only 1,66,591 workers out of 2,62,426 workers in the study area have been provided houses. The rest of the workers (95,835) are yet deprived of getting housing benefits from their employers. Six such tea estates in North Bengal have not at all provided housing facilities to any single worker.

Beach tea estate of Alipurduar has provided the maximum number of houses, i.e., 1,802. Fifty-one tea estates have provided houses to 80 percent or more workmen of their tea estates.

Educational Facilities

Section 14 of the Act prescribes that in case of plantations wherein the total number of children of permanent workers ages between 6 and 12 years is above 25, the appropriate authority may frame rules to provide education in the prescribed standard manner for those children.

It has been noticed that out of a total of 276 tea estates, school facility is available in 231 tea estates in North Bengal. Children of the remaining 45 tea estates have to go to the neighboring schools for learning. Only 143 tea estates provide transportation facilities for school purposes. Tractors and trucks are the common mode of transportation for schoolgoing children.

Recreational Facilities

Section 13 of the Plantation Labour Act prescribes that the planter should arrange recreational facilities for its workers as well as for the children of the workers.

It has been noticed that only 197 tea plantations have made arrangements for the club for the recreation purpose of the workers. In most of the plantations, it has been found that the club is not in good condition and is mostly non-operative. Playground is available in almost all the tea plantations, but the plantation management does not financially support recreational activities. Plantation management is also passive to arrange any kind of sports or games.

Crèches Facilities

According to Section 12 of the Act, an employer should provide crèches facility in every plantation where the number of women workers is 50 or more and these workers may be employed ordinarily or by the contractor, and the number of children of those women workers is 20 or more (aged up to six years).

It has been found that almost every tea estates have crèches except three tea estates. In most of the tea estates, mobile crèches were found to be existent. Crèches have also been found running under tree or tent some-where in the open area beside the plucking plots. The numbers of attendants are very less and they are not well trained. Biscuit and milk are common foods for the children in the crèche. However, only 144 tea estates offer milk in the crèches.

Canteen Facilities

Section 11 of the Act prescribe; the state government may frame regula-tion for those plantations wherein 150 numbers of workers are generally engaged. It is required that one or additional canteen(s) be provided and the maintenance be done by the employer. It has been observed that only 148 tea estates have canteen facilities for their workers, out of which 43 tea estates have subsidized price facilities.

There are some other benefits which are provided to the tea plantation workers. These benefits are non-statutory. Usually, these benefits are pro-vided as per the demand made by labor unions to plantation management. Then plantation management based on their ability provides such facilities to the workers. A brief description of non-statutory benefits for tea workers has presented in the following.

Food Grains

Rice, flour, kerosene oil, etc., as means of ration are provided to the work-ers at concessional prices. In addition to these, workers are also provided a certain quantity of dray tea. Presently, the ration for tea workers is provided by the state government and, to date, it is considered as the component of the wage for tea workers in Bengal.

Fuels (Firewood)

The planters in Bengal offer 2.5 pills of firewood to each worker at free of cost. Usually, branches of the tree, coal, etc. are provided in sufficient quantity for domestic uses once in a year. But this quantity doesn't seem to be enough and the workers have to collect fuel from the nearby jungles.

Umbrella, Tarpaulin, Slipper, and Kambal (Blanket)

Every year before starting of the rainy season, the plantation management provides slipper and umbrella to workers to protect them while they work in the field. Tarpaulin is also provided to the workers for protection while working in the field. Blankets are also provided to the workers. But during the field survey, it was found that in most of the tea estates, such facilities are provided irregularly and the items are not distributed to the workers for a long period.

Existing Welfare Scenario in Tea Estates

To know the actual welfare scenario of tea workers in the North Bengal region, an attempt was made to investigate the sample tea estates of this region. The same methodology (discussed in Chapter 5) has been used in the case of exploring the welfare scenario of tea workers in North Bengal.

With the aid of a well-structured questionnaire, the required primary data has been gathered. The questionnaire has been designed with the prime objective of welfare of tea workers only. Secondary data has been gathered from the publication of Labour Department of Government of West Bengal, Tea Board of India, various research journals, books, etc. However, previous four years' records in terms of welfare expenses have been taken into consideration. Finally, one-way ANOVA technique has been used to draw appropriate conclusions. One-way ANOVA technique has been used to compare the existing welfare scenario among different types of tea companies in the North Bengal region. In the following, stepwise analysis has been presented.

However, for conducting one-way ANOVA, the following assumptions should be satisfied.

I.   DEPENDENT AND INDEPENDENT VARIABLES

The dependent variable should be continuous. In our study, the dependent variable is the previous four years average of welfare expenses. So, this is continuous data. The independent variable should possess various levels. In our study, the independent variable is ownership pattern and it has four levels: i.e., Partnership Company, Public Limited Company, Proprietorship Company, and Public Sector Undertakings. Hence, the first criterion has been met.

II.   TEST OF NORMALITY

The normality test suggests to us whether we will apply a parametric test or nonparametric test. If the data set is somehow normally distributed, then it would be a parametric test, and on the other hand, if the data set is not approximately normally distributed, it would be a nonparametric test.

Ho: Data is normally distributed.

In the case of this study, since we have only 33 respondents, the Shapiro-Wilk test has been followed to check the normality.

In the case of welfare expenses, the calculated p-value of the Shapiro-Wilk test is 0.694, which is above 0.05; so, the null hypothesis is accepted. From the extracted result of the normality test conclusion may be drawn that the data set is somehow normally distributed.

III. HOMOGENEITY OF VARIANCES

Ho: There is no significant difference between the group's variance.

We have conducted Levene's test to check the homogeneity of variances. We have observed the calculated value for Levene's test is 2.507 with a probability value of 0.079. The significant value is more than the generally accepted value of alpha ($p > .05$). Hence, we keep the null hypothesis for the homogeneity of variance. It can be concluded that there are no statistically cabalistic differences among the variances of the four groups.

For conducting the ANOVA, the data set has met the stipulated criteria. Therefore, we have conducted the following analysis.

Analysis of variance (ANOVA)
Hypotheses
Ho: There are no significant differences among the various types of tea plantation company's average welfare expenses in the North Bengal region.
Ha: There are significant differences among the various types of tea plantation company's average welfare expenses in the North Bengal region.

RESULTS OF ANOVA TEST

We have conducted an ANOVA test on the sample data of four groups and we have noticed that the model value of F is 8.499 and the corresponding p value is 0.000, which is smaller than the generally accepted value of p (0.05). Hence, our null hypothesis is discarded and we may infer that there are significant differences among the various types of tea plantation company's average welfare expenses in the North Bengal region.

Post hoc analysis is elaborately described in Table 6.1, specifically where the differences exist.

However, it is detected that the differences exist among Public Limited Tea Companies and Partnership Tea Companies ($p = 0.004$), Public Limited Tea Companies and Public Sector Undertakings Tea Companies ($p = 0.004$), Proprietorship Tea Companies and Partnership Tea Companies ($p = 0.046$), Proprietorship Tea Companies and Public Sector Undertakings Tea Companies ($p = 0.044$). In all cases, the p-value is smaller than 0.05.

Table 6.1 Multiple Comparisons

(I) Ownership	(J) Ownership	Mean Difference (I-J)	Std. Error	Sig.	95% Confidence Interval	
					Lower Bound	Upper Bound
Public	Proprietor	2.90173	1.52893	0.251	−1.2638	7.0673
	Partnership	11.49750*	3.07101	**0.004**	3.1305	19.8645
	PSU	11.54250*	3.07101	**0.004**	3.1755	19.9095
Proprietor	Public	−2.90173	1.52893	0.251	−7.0673	1.2638
	Partnership	8.59577*	3.11013	**0.046**	0.1222	17.0694
	PSU	8.64077*	3.11013	**0.044**	0.1672	17.1144
Partnership	Public	−11.49750*	3.07101	**0.004**	−19.8645	−3.1305
	Proprietor	−8.59577*	3.11013	**0.046**	−17.0694	−0.1222
	PSU	.04500	4.09468	1.000	−11.1110	11.2010
PSU	Public	−11.54250*	3.07101	**0.004**	−19.9095	−3.1755
	Proprietor	−8.64077*	3.11013	**0.044**	−17.1144	−0.1672
	Partnership	−.04500	4.09468	1.000	−11.2010	11.1110

From the statistical examination, it has been noticed that the average amount of expenses on the welfare of tea plantation workers in the study is significantly unequal. The inequality has been established between the Public Limited Tea Company with Partnership Tea Company and Public Sector Undertakings Tea Company, Proprietorship Tea Company with Partnership Tea Company and Public Sector Undertakings Tea Company. This inequality on labor welfare is unexpected while all the tea plantations are operating in the same region and under the same framework of the legislation.

As far as the Plantation Labour Act is concerned, the scenario of welfare benefit has found to be worse. Regarding the housing for the workers, around 36 percent of them are deprived of the said benefits. Talking about the schools, there are no sufficient numbers of teachers. Most of the schools are run and maintained by the state government. The quality of education provided by these schools is abysmally poor. Mode of transportation for the schoolgoing children is also below the standard. Only 148 tea estates have canteen facilities but most of these are not operating smoothly and no price chart has been found. Crèches and recreational facilities are not up to the standard.

References

Bhowmik, S. K. (1981). *Class formation in the plantation system*. New Delhi, India: People's Publishing House, p. 109.

Das, A. K. (2009). *Sustainability in tea industry: An Indian perspective; the social scanner*. New Delhi, India: Akansha Publishing House.

Duara, M. (2015). *Evolving intricacies of industrial relations: A study of selected tea estates in Assam* (Doctoral thesis), IIT- Guwahati, Guwahati, India, p. 44. Retrieved from: http://gyan.iitg.ernet.in/handle/123456789/596

Flippo, E. B. (1984). *Personnel management*. New York, US: McGraw-Hill.

Ghosh, A. K. (2006). *Human resource management*. New Delhi, India: Manas Publications.

Government of West Bengal. (2013). *Synopsis on survey of tea gardens*. Kolkata, India: State Labour Institute, p. 5.

Mitra, D. (2010). *Globalization and industrial relations in tea plantations*. New Delhi, India: Abhijeet Publication, pp. 47, 96–98.

NRPPD. (2015). *Wage mobility and labour market institutions in tea plantations: The case of West Bengal and Assam* (Discussion Paper—46). Thiruvananthapuram, Indian: Sarkar, K., p. 15.

Prasanneswari. (1984). Industrial relation in tea plantation: The Dooars scene. *Economic and Political Weekly*, 19(24/25), pp. 956–959.

7 Findings, Conclusions, and Recommendations

Major Findings

The major findings of the study are as follows:

Recruitment and Selection of the Tea Workers

i. From the study, it has been found that the number of permanent job positions remains the same in tea plantation over the years. No new job position has been created in tea plantation.

ii. Recruitment in tea plantation has been made only on account of the death of a permanent worker or enduringly leaves the job by the permanent worker and replacement is made accordingly.

iii. One of the peculiar issues in the recruitment of tea workers is that the legal heir gets the job of the deceased person or the person who leaves job permanently. For replacement in job, only family members get job in those positions.

iv. On special occasions, fresh recruitment is done rarely on the non-availability of the legal heir of the deceased person or the person who leaves the job permanently. This is done in consultation with the unions.

v. The study found that the recruitment of *Bigha* workers is made during the peak season only. The study also found that *Bigha* workers are recruited from within and outside of tea estates.

vi. The study revealed that physical fitness is the prime criterion for the recruitment of permanent as well as for the *Bigha* workers.

vii. The study further confirmed that the traditional and conventional methods of recruitment systems are being followed by the tea plantations in the study region.

Training and Development of the Tea Workers

i. Our study found that training is crucial for the tea workers. The tea plantation industry is one of the labor-concentrated industries. Therefore, a huge quantum of labor is necessary all over the year for nurturing tea plants and for the manufacturing process of tea.

ii. The study has established that only 36 percent, i.e., in 12 out of 33 sample tea estates, have training provision for their workers.

iii. Proprietorship Tea Company occupies the topmost position in terms of the training program offered. Under this company, 7 sample tea estates have training provision out of 13 sample tea estates which were surveyed, i.e., about 53.84 percent.

iv. Our study has identified that the Public Sector Undertaking Tea Company has no training provision for its workers.

v. Coaching and mentoring modes of training are mostly preferred by the workers' community. This mode of training is offered by almost 42 percent of the sample tea estates.

vi. The study has established that the training program offered by the Proprietorship Tea Company and Partnership Tea Company has some positive effects. The overall performance of the worker before training and after training varies largely.

vii. The training program offered by the Public Limited Tea Company is not statistically important. The overall performance of the worker before and after attaining training remains the same.

Wages of the Tea Workers

i. In the tea industry of Bengal, the wage rate is fixed through the peculiar negotiation process in the presence of three parties, i.e., representatives from planters' associations, representatives of trade unions, and government officials.

ii. Wage fixation for tea workers is done once in three years. The amount of wage fixation for a particular period is usually payable in three installments after the settlement of wage rate through a memorandum of understanding.

iii. Our study has found that between 2001 and 2011, the amount of wage growth rate was confined below 10 percent.

iv. Unanticipated changes in wage growth rate have been found in the year 2012 (13.18 percent) and in the year 2015 (18.4 percent).

v. The study has unveiled a piece of genuine evidence for the drastic changes in wage rate due to political influences. In 2011, there was an assembly election in Bengal and the political condition was in deep turmoil, and consequently, no change was noticed in tea workers' wages during that year. In 2012, the then ruling government increased the wage rate, i.e., 13.18 percent, to acquire good faith of the tea workers. Again, before the assembly election of 2016, a historic wage growth rate, i.e., 18.4 percent, was made in 2015.

vi. The study has established that the wage growth rate for tea workers in North Bengal is directly linked with political influence.

vii. The study further confirms that the overall trend of wage growth rate follows typical randomness. This randomness has been justified by the Run test.

viii. Wage issue is the prime reason for the sudden strikes, closure, and lock-out in the tea estates of this region, making tea industry vulnerable.

Welfare of the Tea Workers

i. In terms of the welfare facilities of tea workers, Public Limited Tea Company stands in the apex position followed by the Proprietorship Tea Company, Partnership Tea Company, and Public Sector Undertakings Tea Company.

ii. In terms of welfare facilities, our study confirms the existence of a statistical momentous difference between Public Limited Tea Company and Partnership Tea Company ($p = 0.004$), Public Limited Tea Company and Public Sector Undertakings Tea Company ($p = .004$), Proprietorship Tea Company, and Partnership Tea Company ($p = 0.046$), Proprietorship Tea Company and Public Sector Undertakings Tea Company ($p = 0.044$).

Conclusions

Tea is the means of sustenance of people in the Northern division of Bengal, where the outsize of tea gardens is located on the foothill areas of Terai, Darjeeling, and Dooars. The tea industry of Bengal has a long history of more than 160 years. It has outspread the entire socio-economic and socio-cultural features of all classes of people of this part of Bengal.

North Bengal occupies the second leading tea-producing province in India, next only to Assam. North Bengal holds 276 tea estates in aggregate. Among the 276 tea estates in Bengal, nearly 150 tea estates are located in the Dooars region, which is one of the principal tea-producing regions in India. In Darjeeling, 81 tea estates are located and this tea-growing region is renowned all over the world for its unique Darjeeling superiority of tea. The rest 45 tea estates are located across the Terai region in West Bengal.

We have performed a methodical study to investigate the 'Human Resource Management practices in the Indian Tea Industry'. Every functional aspect of human resource management, viz. procurement, training and development, compensation, integration, and maintenance, has been discussed in the purview of the tea industry. Our study considers only the labor components of human resources in the tea plantation industry of Bengal, because labor is the heart and soul of tea industry. Our study has found that every functional aspect of human resource management in the tea plantation industry of Bengal is not up to the standard. From the perspectives of recruitment and selection, the traditional and conventional system of labor recruitment and selection has been experiential. Training is offered only by 36 percent sample tea estates. There are no formal ways of appraising the performances of workers. The amount of wage paid to workers is abysmally low and is not justifiable. Even, the amount of wage is not as per the prescribed minimum rate of wage for agricultural workers in the state. The rate of wage is determined through a tripartite agreement where employers' role is influential. Working conditions in terms of working hours and overtime hours are entirely worse following the standard which has been set by the Plantation Labour Act, 1951. Various statutory and non-statutory benefits for labor are unavailable since long. Finally, considerable disparities have also been observed among various types of tea plantation companies on health, safety, and welfare facilities.

However, all these issues have been emerged in the tea plantation industry of Bengal mainly due to the ill effects of liberalization, privatization, and globalization (LPG), which was initiated in India in the year 1991. However, the factual effect of it on the tea industry began from 1998 onward. The Indian tea industry has confronted stiff competition in the global market due to the lessening of the import tariff barrier and withdrawal of the quantity ceiling on import. Thus, to remain competitive in the economy, tea-producing companies of the Bengal have been forced to sink various costs, especially the labor cost. Due to the cost diminution policy, tea-producing companies in this province are not in a position to execute their responsibilities, such as health, welfare, safety, working conditions, etc., to the workers in conformity with the Plantation Labour Act (PLA), 1951. Besides these, inappropriate staffing, passive attitudes of planters on providing proper training, abnormality in payment of wages, bonus, gratuity, provident fund, etc. have been enlarged significantly. Further, other non-statutory benefits for workers like fuels, umbrella, slippers, tarpaulin, etc. have been fully eroded.

Thus, the study concludes that the labor forces, i.e., human resources, are not properly managed in the tea plantation industry in Bengal. As a result, workers who are engaged with the tea industry for the survival of themselves and their families have been unfavorably affected. As a consequence, workers, backed by the trade union, call a strike to create stress on the management to execute their demands. Hence, labor conflict has become a usual phenomenon in this region. Finally, all these issues lead to labor turbulence in the forms of strikes, gheraos, etc. and thus the industry has become vulnerable.

Recommendations

To manage human resources effectively in the tea plantation industry, some suggestions are furnished hereunder:

i. The study established that the actual scenario of the span of control in tea plantations of the North Bengal region is poor. It is suggested that the span of control should be strong.

ii. In the study, it was found that no permanent recruitment took place in tea plantations of the study region except on account of the death of permanent workers, permanently left out the jobs, etc. cases. It is highly recommended that instead of recruitment of casual (*Bigha*) workers, permanent workers should be recruited because job accountability is comparatively more in the case of permanent workers. As we know, for proper nurturing of tea plants and other related activities, responsible workforces are required. So, the recruitment of permanent workers is the best suitable means.

iii. The traditional and conventional system of labor recruitment should be avoided. Further, family-based recruitment is also to be removed.

iv. In the study, we have found that 64 percent of sample tea plantations have no scope of training for their workers. It is highly recommended that tea planters should immediately take necessary actions to organize training.

v. The study has found that for the case of Public Limited Tea Company, the training program was not effective: i.e., the performance of workers remained the same before and after attaining training. It is suggested that at the time of designing the training program, due concentration should be given. The training module should be designed keeping in view the capacity of the learners.

vi. Priority should be given to on-the-job' training methods for workers. Hence, learning while doing would be the best training procedure for tea plantation workers because they are not educated adequately.

vii. Ethical Tea Partnership (ETP) is now an emerging issue in the global tea market. To capture the global market, membership of ETP is highly recommended. Tea workers are the heart and soul of the tea industry.

The employer needs to be aware of the codes of ETP. Training is the only weapon in the hands of the planters to make it possible.

viii. Wage determination should not be left through the negotiation process. Rather, like in South Indian tea plantations, wages should be declared by the government and should be revised from time to time as per the changes in the index numbers through notifications under the Minimum Wages Act, 1948. Minimum wage, however, at least ensures survival at the subsistence level.

ix. During the negotiation courses, the actual representation on behalf of the worker should take part. The so called 'Neta' (Leader) should be avoided during negotiation.

x. In the study, it has been found that the determination of wage to large extent is influenced by political issues. Political issues should be kept aside while determining the rate of daily wages of tea workers.

xi. The amount of wage should be paid on time so that the plantation workers can use the amount for their daily needs. Cash mode of wage payment should be preferred because banking infrastructure is too poor in the adjoining areas where tea gardens are located.

xii. Working conditions for workers in terms of working hours and overtime hours should be justified. Extra work hours should be calculated based on the standard measures, i.e., as per the Plantation Labour Act, for an extra payment.

xiii. Parity should be maintained among all types of tea companies regarding the rate of payment on extra work performed by the workers.

xiv. Inequalities in welfare, health, and safety benefits of tea workers have been found among different categories of tea companies in the study regions. It is suggested that such discriminations should not be there in the same industry and a similar region.

xv. In the lion's portion of tea plantations, it has been found that non-statutory benefits like fuels, umbrella, slippers, tarpaulin, etc. have been eroded. Tea planters should supply this protective equipment regularly so that the workers can be protected bodily during work.

xiv. Efforts to provide secondary schools at every estate should be set as an immediate goal. The Centre of Vocational training should also be set up. They are highly required for future generations of the labor community.

xvii. Appropriate execution of the Plantation Labour Act, 1951, in all aspects for the tea plantation workers is instantly necessary.

xviii. Owners of tea plantations should be awakened by the Tea Board of India about their importance and existence in terms of job creator, pioneer of economic development, the sustainability of the industry, environment, and ecology, so that effective entrepreneurial values may emerge in themselves.

xix. The quality of the tea bush impacts the market price of tea. The quality of the tea bush depends on proper nurturing and care. Labor of tea plantations is responsible for caring and nurturing the tea bushes. Hence, plantation management should pay adequate attention to its labor.

xx. It is highly recommended that restrictions should be made by the appropriate authority on frequent change of ownership of tea estates of this region because the frequent change of ownership results in fewer responsibilities and obligations on labor by the owners.

xxi. Lastly, the roles of the Tea Board of India (TBI) and the state government should be more active on the performance of tea plantations.

Glossary

ACMS—Assam Cha Mazdur Sangh
AITUC—All India Trade Union Congress
ANOVA—Analysis of variance
BMI—Body mass index
BMS—Bhartiya Mazdoor Sangh
CBMU—Cha Bagan Mazdur Union
CITU—Centre of Indian Trade Union
CPI—Consumer price index
CTC—Curl, tear, and curl
DA—Dearness Allowance
DBITA—Doors Branch of Indian Tea Association
DBITA—Dooars Branch of Indian Tea Association
ETP—Ethical Tea Partnership
FERA—Foreign Exchange Regulations Act
HMS—Hind Mazdur Sabha
ILO—International Labour Organization
INTUC—Indian National Trade Union Congress
IR—Industrial relations
ITA—Indian Tea Association
ITPA—Indian Tea Planters Association
LO—Labour officers
LWO—Labour welfare officers
LPG—Liberalization, privatization, and globalization
NBMR—North Bengal Mounted Rifles
NCL—National Commission on Labour
NEITPBA—North East India Tea Plantation Bonus Agreement
NILM—National Institutes of Labour Management
NTUC—National Trade Union Congress
NTUF—National Trade Unions Federation
NUPW—National United of Plantation Workers

PLA—Plantation Labour Act
SPSS—Statistical Package for Social Sciences
STG—Small tea growers
TBI—Tea Board of India
UK—United Kingdom
UPASI—United Planters Association of South India
WBCSU—West Bengal Cha Sramik Union

Index

Note: Page numbers in *italics* indicate a figure and page numbers in **bold** indicate a table on the corresponding page.